WESTERN
HUNTING GUIDE

*A Complete Where-To-Go & How-To-Do-It
Guide to Western Hunting*

By Mike Lapinski

Western Hunting Guide

ISBN 0912299-43-6 (Hardcover)
ISBN 0912299-44-4 (Softcover)

Cover Photo: Author Mike Lapinski caught this bull elk at rest in a majestic setting in the Rocky Mountains. The bull elk symbolizes both the awesome size and the majesty of the American West.

STONEYDALE PRESS PUBLISHING COMPANY
205 Main Street — Drawer B
Stevensville, Montana 59870
Phone: 406-777-2729

Table of Contents

Dedication

Then God said, "Let us make Man in our image, and after our likeness; and let them have dominion over the fish of the sea, and over the birds of the air, and over the cattle, and over all the earth, and over every creeping thing that creeps upon the earth." — Genesis 1:26

Introduction

The Rocky Mountains in the western United States rise skyward from Montana in the north to New Mexico in the south. This magnificent mountain range is breathtakingly beautiful, with its lofty snow-capped peaks and alpine meadows in the high country, sloping down to heavy coniferous forests and streams in the lower country. And to the west of the Rockies lies the Cascade Range, a smaller, but equally breathtaking string of rugged mountains.

But for all their grandeur, the western forests harbor an even greater wealth, especially for the sportsman. Large and diversified herds of big game animals such as mule and whitetail deer, elk, moose, grizzly and black bear, antelope, sheep, goats, and lion still abound in the western states

Sportsmen who experience the hunt in the western wilderness are usually changed for life. They are humbled by the endless spectacular natural beauty of the land, and they experience exhilarating hunting that makes the blood rush through their veins in red hot excitement.

Wisconsin resident Bob Mussey reflected on his bowhunt for elk in the rugged Montana high country. Bob said, "There will always be a special place in my heart for my high country hunt for rutting bull elk. Talk about close encounters! It was an experience I'll never forget. I can relive it anytime, anywhere, just by closing my eyes."

Beside being beautiful, the western states are just plain vast. This is a land where counties are often larger than some eastern states, where human populations are still numbered at a couple of people per square mile!

It is indeed a big land, and that is the first thing that the visiting urban hunter notices. Those large big game herds are spread throughout this seemingly endless land that is sometimes open, but more often brushy and timbered, or rocky, or near vertical. Beautiful yes, but also tough to hunt, and often tougher to find game.

Every year a small army of nonresident hunters from every corner of the country makes their dream hunt to the western states. Some come prepared and the result is a successful big game hunt with huge elk racks and exciting stories to take back home.

Other hunters are not fully prepared when they make their western big game hunt, and they often are bewildered that huge bull elk or trophy mule deer are not found behind every tree. In fact, it is not unusual for an unprepared hunting party to hunt hard for two weeks and leave not only with no trophies, but also without even seeing an elk!

The secret ingredient to a successful western hunting experience is planning. The smart hunter who carefully plans his western dream hunt may live 3,000 miles from the Rockies, but he will have a good idea of where the animals will be found in the area he'll be hunting long before he makes the trip.

The smart hunter will also know what type of vehicle, camping gear, and clothing to use in his particular area of the West. If he decides to make a guided hunt, his careful planning will have pinpointed the best guides for the type of animal he wants to hunt. If he is after a trophy, he will know in advance which states, and more specifically, which areas of those states harbor the top trophy animals.

It is neither the perfect stalk, nor the true flight of the arrow or bullet that insures the success of the hunt. The successful hunt was begun months earlier when the smart hunter made careful plans concerning the "what, why, where, when, and how" of his upcoming big game hunt that ultimately caused his dream hunt to live up to its expectations.

Before a hunter begins to oil his favorite rifle or tune his bow in anticipation of the big hunt, he must first sit down and ask those basic questions: What do I want to hunt? Why do I want to hunt it? Where do I want to hunt? When? How?

They are simple questions, but the effort that a sportsman makes in finding the correct answers for himself may spell the difference between the success and failure of his western dream hunt.

Careful planning can also save a prospective western big game hunter money. While some big game species in the West are best hunted with a good guide, other species can be hunted adequately without a guide. And careful research into that murky area of choosing a good outfitter will ultimately pay off not only monetarily, but also with top quality service.

This book is dedicated to sportsmen everywhere who have a burning desire to make a successful western big game hunt in the Rocky Mountains. It covers all the necessary planning and preparations needed to make either a guided or an unguided hunt.

Chapter Two will be especially helpful for the nonresident. It points out the best western state to hunt for each game species, thereby greatly increasing a hunter's chances for success. It also notes which state offers the greatest trophy hunting potential for each species.

In addition, Appendix A includes an exhaustive scouting report on every big game species found in the primary western hunting states of Arizona, Colorado, Idaho, Montana, Nevada, New Mexico, Oregon, Utah, Washington, and Wyoming.

Appendix A provides detailed information on where the best areas are in each western state. With this information in hand, even a sportsman living on the other side of the world will have a good start towards finding that special mountain or drainage where his dream hunt will take place.

Mike Lapinski
Superior, Montana
July 15, 1988

A hunter's moon hangs over this feeding bull elk.

Chapter 1

THE DECISION TO MAKE YOUR WESTERN DREAM HUNT

Sportsmen as far back as Teddy Roosevelt were lured to the western Rocky Mountains by the adventure and excitement of the hunt. They went because they'd heard glowing accounts of breathtaking scenery and strange, exotic big game to hunt.

Today's sportsman feels that same irresistible call of the western wilderness as a result of exciting hunting tales passed on by friends or from articles in outdoor magazines. He is lured by that American pioneer spirit and quest for adventure that brought the mountain men west 150 years ago.

Actually, a hunter today has more reason to make a western hunt than his predecessors. Much of our forests and hunting lands in urban states are rapidly shrinking due to the advance of civilization, and the urban hunter is sometimes hard pressed to find a place to hunt deer. I know the feeling. By the time I left Pennsylvania in 1970, it was difficult to find a tract of woods that was not posted.

I remember how discouraging it was to stumble among the hordes of hunters on the first day of buck season in New York. There were so many hunters that the deer rarely left their sanctuaries in deep thickets, and more often than not, I went through the entire hunting season without seeing a buck.

On the other hand, the western Rocky Mountain states are primarily national forest. Any sportsman holding a valid state hunting license can hunt there without worrying about posted signs or someone kicking him off the land.

Being a transplanted easterner, I never tired of watching the great enjoyment that hunters from urban areas felt when they looked out across endless miles of western wilderness that was theirs as much as it's yours.

Every sportsman deserves the opportunity to hunt trophy animals in the West where hunting pressure is often nonexistent.

Many hunters tell me that this experience was worth the hunting trip in itself!

Another reason to make a western big game hunting trip is the amazing variety of big game found in the western states. These are the critters that most hunters only dream of. Huge elk and moose, surly grizzly and black bears, mule and whitetail deer, antelope, sheep, goats, and lion comprise a tantalizing array of big game that is sure to provide great sport for the hunter.

Every sportsman in America deserves that one hunt where there isn't another hunter behind every bush, where the game is exotic and plentiful, where the hunter can roam freely and stalk big game in a solitary forest. If that sounds like a great way to hunt, you've just made the decision to go west.

Plan About A Year Ahead

It is best to give yourself about a year lead time before your hunting trip. It's surprising how many time consuming details are involved in a western big game hunt. In particular, license applications, outfitters, and vacation time are areas of planning that require a great amount of lead time. Even if a group of hunters chooses to hunt without an outfitter, a lot of time must be spent making contacts and writing letters to faraway states in

Give yourself a year to plan your western dream hunt. Take your time and study hunting potential, outfitters, and statistics before making the final choice.

order to locate a prime hunting area.

Big game licenses in some western states go on sale the first of the year, while other western states make theirs available in March. Sale of these nonresident licenses is brisk and most are usually sold out by June. Consequently, the hunter who gets the sudden urge to make a western hunt in the spring would probably not be able to get enough other men together to submit nonresident applications in time to make a western hunt that fall.

Outfitters especially must be contacted a year in advance, and some of the more popular ones have a two year waiting list. Besides, this is one area where a client should move cautiously and not get in too much of a rush. Therefore, it is best to use that year-long wait before the hunt to contact and check references and credentials of particular outfitters.

Don't Put Off Your Western Hunt

Once you make the decision to go on a western big game hunt, don't get cold feet and put it off for a couple of years. The best time to go is within a year of your decision. In other words, as soon as possible.

While it is true that the western Rocky Mountains are a vast expanse of wilderness, their treasured wildlife resource is receiving increasing pressure every year from hunter demand plus the encroachment of

Don't put off your western dream hunt too long. The West is constantly changing, and increased pressure on the land and its wildlife make it imperative to go as soon as possible.

civilization. Some western states that only a few years ago allowed either-sex elk hunting for two months in the fall now limit elk hunting to bulls-only for a few weeks.

Right now, big game herds in the west are healthy, and a license is not too costly or difficult to obtain. But who knows what it will be like five or 10 years from now? Don't put off your western dream hunt until the kids are grown up or you retire. Life is too short to plan that far ahead. The best time to make your hunt is as soon as possible.

Cost Of A Western Hunt

The cost of a western big game hunt is probably one of the biggest stumbling blocks for a sportsman. And the biggest trap that a guy can fall into in this area is when he begins to weigh the value of a western hunting trip against the dollar outlay.

Many fellow outfitters that I've talked to on this subject agree that a client's worry over the cost of a western big game hunt is one the biggest reasons why a nonresident's dream hunt ends in a nightmare. Montana outfitter Harvey Mead commented, "Some guys start worrying about how much money they're losing if they don't kill anything the first day out!"

The challenge and excitement of a western hunt comes from the fact that the game is both cunning and elusive. And success is not a foregone conclusion.

The eastern urban hunter who hunts mostly with rifled slugs can save money by borrowing a rifle to hunt certain western game such as the antelope.

Harvey added, "I tell them long before they come out west to forget the money they put aside for their hunt. Consider it gone forever. That way they can enjoy the positive things of their hunt without putting a price tag on it."

Another money problem that I've encountered as a guide is a client's increasing surliness if he does not kill game as the hunt winds down. This is usually because the guy had the misconception that the western forests are so full of big game that all a hunter needs to do is walk outdoors, pick his animal, and drop it.

The challenge and excitement of the hunt comes from the fact that the quarry is both cunning and elusive. That's why we call it a sport — because the result is not a foregone conclusion. Consequently, a hunter should not gauge the success or failure of his western hunt by whether or not he brings back a trophy.

The cost of a western big game hunt varies, depending on what type of hunt is planned and what species of game is hunted. A hunter who books a fully guided hunt for trophy bull elk in the Bob Marshall Wilderness of Montana will have to pay much more money than the hunter who hunts antelope on his own in eastern Wyoming.

The guided hunter avoids the difficulties of field dressing and the excruciating chore of packing out game.

Of course, that's not to say that an unguided western hunt is dirt cheap. The unguided hunters must still pay a healthy price for a nonresident hunting license. In addition, they will have the cost of hunting transportation, lodging, food, specialized equipment, plus an emergency reserve of cash in case the vehicle breaks down.

An average group of three sportsmen from the East Coast should expect to pay about $1,200 each for an unguided elk hunt in Idaho. That figure begins to drop the further west that these prospective hunters live, due to savings in transportation cost. Also, if the hunters pursue less exotic game such as mule deer or antelope, expenses drop some more because the license cost for these species is lower.

The guided hunter avoids the problems and cost of food, lodging, and hunting transportation, but he must pay for the services of an outfitter. Guiding fees vary between outfitters, but generally a hunter can expect to pay about $3,000 for a 10-day guided hunt, or $1,800 for a 5-day hunt.

This might seem like a lot of money, but actually a western expedition is one of the cheapest big game hunts available in the world when you consider that a moose hunt in Canada might run upwards to $10,000, and an Alaska guided hunt can cost even more!

Below is a breakdown of the cost for a typical guided and unguided Idaho elk hunt for a party of three hunters from the east:

	Unguided Hunt (seven days)	5-day Guided Hunt	10-day Guided Hunt
License	$400	$400	$400
Trans.	$300	$300	$300
Lodging	$200	$0	$0
Food	$200	$0	$0
Misc. Supplies	$100	$0	$0
Guide Fee	$0	$1800	$3000
Total	**$1200**	**$2500**	**$3700**

Savings Tips

One of the best ways to save money on a western trip is to include several hunters. The cost of transportation, lodging, and food drop sharply with each additional man. Even a guided hunt will be less expensive because an outfitter usually gives a discount for groups.

Another savings tip for hunters making an unguided trip is to bring along your own lodging in the form of a travel trailer or tent. Motel lodging even in the west is expensive, and so are restaurant meals. Besides, hunters usually enjoy the western wilderness experience more when they stay out in the bush where they are hunting.

Here's another money saving tip. Don't go out and buy every single

The cost of typical guided elk hunt today is about $3,000. Weigh the benefits of a guided hunt against the lower cost of an unguided hunt.

special accessory that is needed for your western trip. When you begin purchasing things such as tents, trailers, gas stoves, etc., you will quickly run up a large bill. Instead, try to borrow or rent most of this equipment.

One particularly large expenditure that some hunters may be able to avoid is the cost of a specialized big game rifle for western hunting. In the area of southern New York where I hunted, only shotguns using rifled slugs were allowed for deer hunting, and most hunters did not own a large calibre rifle suitable for long range big game hunting. Consequently, any sportsman who wanted to make a big game hunting trip to the west had to purchase a high powered rifle, say in .300 magnum calibre, that he could not even use back home.

An alternative to this dilemma is to get a loan of an adequate high powered rifle from an acquaintance. I realize that it is supposed to be a poor practice to hunt with a borrowedd gun, but I have had several clients who used loaned rifles and did well with them.

The biggest problem with using a loaned rifle is that the hunter is unfamiliar with the weapon. However, if a hunter practices with this loaned rifle until he is competent, he can not only make the tough hunting shots but he can also save upwards to $500 by avoiding the purchase of a new rifle that he might have no other use for.

Chapter 2

CHOOSING THE ANIMAL AND THE STATE TO HUNT

A sportsman planning a western hunt may choose which animal he wants to hunt and which state to hunt it in for one or more reasons. Ever since I was old enough to hunt, I wanted to hunt elk, and I read every bit of information that I could get my hands on concerning elk. I was fascinated by the huge size, enormous rack, and the high country habitat of the elk, so when I made my first western hunt, it should come as no surprise that my heart was set on a bull elk.

Other men are more interested in the special sport associated with a particular animal. George Schultz and his two hunting partners from Pennsylvania have made two western hunts, and they never got any further west than the Wyoming prairie. All three men are woodchuck hunters, and they enjoy lightweight, flat shooting firearms. Consequently, they love to hunt antelope, and when you mention the challenge of the bull elk to them, they just kind of blink back at you in disbelief.

But whatever species you decide upon, you should at least be aware of which states provide the best hunting for that species. Actually, it is difficult in some cases to identify which state is the "best" because several factors must be weighed. The four most important factors to look for in your search for the right state are: (1) the size or harvest of the game herd, (2) the best chance for success, (3) difficulty in obtaining a license, (4) trophy potential.

But keep in mind that the top state for a particular species may be in the eye of the beholder. Take elk hunting as an example. No doubt about it, Colorado is tops in elk population, total kill, and hunter success, and a sportsman who simply wants to hunt elk may be attracted to that state. But the hunter who is after a big bull elk will counter that Montana is not that far behind Colorado in those categories, and it far surpasses that state in record book trophies. But another guy will add that Arizona is the

Colorado is the top rated western state for elk.

Idaho is the sleeper for trophy elk.There are lots of big bulls roaming the backcountry of this rugged state, but remember that most of Idaho has steep, brushy terrain.

leading state by far for record book entries verses total elk harvest.

Below is a narrative comparison, by species, of all eight major western big game hunting states and how they stack-up against each other, beginning with the top state. But keep in mind that the top state for a particular species may be in the eye of the beholder.

ELK

Colorado

Colorado is the top rated western state for elk hunting, with a large herd of 155,000 animals, and an annual kill rate of about 30,000 elk annually. In addition, many nonresidents find Colorado's licensing system attractive because every applicant who sends in their money gets a license, so there is no nail biting while you wait to see if your dream hunt must be postponed because you weren't drawn for a tag.

As a result of these attractive figures, Colorado is heavily hunted. About 200,000 hunters crowd into the prime elk hunting areas every fall, and hunter success is about 12% — decent, but not great.

The hunter who just wants to hunt elk and is not concerned with bringing home a big trophy bull should find Colorado a good elk hunting state.

Wyoming is well known for its trophy elk hunting, second only to Montana in record book bull elk.

But the guy who has his heart set on a place where his chances of killing a big bull are good, might want to explore what other western elk states have to offer. Don't get me wrong, there are some big bulls in Colorado, but they are mostly located in the very rugged backcountry where hunting pressure is light, and most nonresidents will never get to.

However, there is some good news concerning Colorado's status for trophy bull elk hunting. A few years ago, the state set new regulations banning the killing of spike bulls in the prime Wind River country of northwestern Colorado. By now, this attempt to upgrade the size of the average bull elk should be paying off, and the potential for killing a branch antlered bull should be much better than the poor reputation that Colorado currently has as a trophy elk state.

Montana

Montana is recognized as the top western elk state for trophy bulls, with 52 entries in the Boone & Crockett record book. The Big Sky State has a large, well-dispersed elk herd of about 150,000 animals, and hunters kill about 15,000 elk annually.

The elk herd is so well-dispersed that hunting pressure never gets so intense that hunters feel crowded. As a resident of this state, I'm surprised that several very productive elk areas that I know of hardly even see a hunter all season. Elk hunting in these lightly hunted areas is excellent because the potential for finding a trophy sized bull is much better, and the hunting itself is better because the elk are less wary.

A drawback to elk hunting in Montana has been its first-come, first-served policy of issuing the 17,000 nonresident combination licenses (elk, deer, bear). In the past, there has been a mad rush for these licenses, but recently, this logjam has been easing and any nonresident who is prompt can expect to receive a license. In addition, Montana now allows a special antelope & deer license for nonresidents who don't want to hunt elk, thereby leaving those combination licenses for folks who are primarily after elk.

Oregon

Oregon ranks second to Colorado in total elk harvest, with an annual kill of about 20,000 out of a healthy herd of 93,000 animals. But those figures lose some of their luster when you consider that Oregon has only six bulls listed in the Boone & Crockett record book. In addition, the bull-cow ratio in some heavily hunted areas is very low, four bulls per 100 cows. Also, the prime elk hunting areas receive intense hunting pressure.

Consequently, you would have to consider Oregon to be a good state to hunt for elk, but not for trophy elk. I showed this assessment to an Oregon friend of mine, and he snickered. "Great," he told me, "I'll have all that good elk hunting to myself!"

Idaho

Idaho is in the middle of the pack, with a yearly harvest of about 11,000 elk out of a herd of 106,000. There are 25 Idaho elk entered in the Boone & Crockett record book, and I believe that this state is a "sleeper" for trophy elk. I hunt there every year, and I can personally attest to the fact that there are still lots of trophy sized bulls roaming within a mile of public highways.

Idaho is passed over by many elk hunters because of its difficult terrain. Typical Idaho elk terrain is very steep and rugged, with heavy brush. Consequently, hunters with physical limitations should be careful where they plan their Idaho hunt. There are a few elk areas with moderate terrain, but not many. In fact, the brush continues right up to timberline in some areas, thereby limiting visibility and increasing frustration.

Wyoming

Wyoming is another state in the middle of the pack, with an annual elk

Any way you look at it, Colorado is tops for trophy mule deer hunting.

kill of about 15,000 from a herd of 70,000 animals. However, Wyoming is well known for its trophy elk hunting, with 42 bulls in the record book, second only to Montana, and it has the overall highest hunting success rate of about 30%.

However, Wyoming is burdened by two bewildering laws which greatly hinder its rise to the top for nonresident elk hunting. First, it issues all of its nonresident elk tags on a lottery basis. Consequently, you must keep all of your elk hunting plans on hold until you find out if you were drawn for a license — your chances are about 50-50.

The second problem area is the law that requires nonresidents who hunt the wilderness areas, where much of the top elk hunting is located, to use a guide. No problem if that's what you'd planned to begin with, but if you want a self-guided hunt, be careful to plan your hunt in a non-wilderness area.

Wyoming is spectacularly beautiful country, with huge, steep mountains and high country meadows. It's also taxing for the hunter with physical limitations, so be careful to pick an area with moderate steepness if you are not able to hike through steep, rugged terrain.

Washington

Washington has some decent statistics concerning elk. Hunters kill about 11,000 animals every year from a herd of about 60,000. However, the success ratio is a slim 7% and there are only two Yellowstone elk in the Boone & Crockett record book. This is due to the limited range of the elk herd, which is confined to pockets of prime habitat where large numbers of hunters often create unbearable hunting pressure.

There are some bright spots for Washington elk hunting. Much of the mountainous elk terrain in Washington is moderate, and there is even some flat ground elk hunting done in the northeast and West Coast areas, so a hunter with physical limitations could find many suitable elk hunting areas. In addition, the elk hunting in the mountains of Washington is done at moderate elevations of about 3,000 feet, which may be more attractive to the hunter who might have problems with thin air.

Arizona

Arizona has about 18,000 elk, and hunters take 1,900 of them every year. Because of these numbers, Arizona is not considered to be a top elk state overall. But in this case, numbers are a bit deceiving.

Arizona grows big elk! Considering its relatively small elk harvest, there are a whopping 18 elk in the Boone & Crockett record book, and the chances of a hunter killing a trophy elk are excellent.

Unfortunately, a hunter must first obtain a license, and competition is fierce. In addition, much of the elk hunting in Arizona is on private ran-

The Idaho/Utah border has a reputation for producing good size mule deer bucks.

ches or Indian reservations which charge healthy hunting fees and tightly control the number of permits to insure quality hunting. That's the secret of all the big bull elk in Arizona, which is not a bad idea.

Any hunter who wants the best chance to take a top elk trophy should consider Arizona. Sure, you might need a little patience when applying for a license, but remember, Arizona has by far more record book elk than any other state when you take into consideration its total harvest.

Arizona is another state that offers elk hunters with limitations some moderate hunting ground. Some of it is high country, park-like terrain, but there are some moderate slopes even up high that are physically easy to hunt.

New Mexico

New Mexico has an elk herd of about 15,000 with an annual harvest of about 2,000 and 11% success rate. Competition is tough for the limited number of elk licenses issued, and officials are determined to slowly bring all public elk hunting up to trophy level. In fact, several huge ranches and Indian reservations now offer limited hunting which offers exceptional trophy potential. Of course, competition is also stiff for these permits, and the cost of this private hunting is high.

New Mexico hunting is mostly at high elevations, but the terrain is not too steep. Consequently, a hunter who has physical limitations, but could handle the thin air, could do well in New Mexico.

Nevada & Utah

Elk hunting is very limited in these states and most nonresidents pass them over.

MULE DEER

Colorado

Any way you look at it, Colorado is the top state by far for mule deer. Colorado's muley population of 500,000 animals is tops in the west, and its hunter success rate of 34% is right up there with the best in the west.

But the most astounding statistic concerning Colorado mule deer hunting is the fact that it has 221 entries in the Boone & Crockett record book. In fact, over 35% of all mule deer entries in the record book come from Colorado.

Another nice thing about Colorado is their licensing system for nonresidents. Send in your money and you get a license. No hoping and nail biting with this state!

Idaho has the best black bear hunting in the West.

Utah

Utah has a mule deer population of 500,000 and hunters harvest about 70,000 animals annually for a 32% success rate. In addition, Utah also has 57 entries in the Boone & Crockett record book. These statistics prove that Utah is a good place to hunt big mule deer in the west.

Wyoming

Wyoming has a mule deer population of 400,000, and hunters annually harvest about 55,000 animals for a success rate of 60%. On the down side, Wyoming lags a bit behind some other states in the record book with 46 entries. However, local residents who know all the favorite haunts of the big muley bucks assure me that there are big bucks to be had in Wyoming, and lots of them!

Idaho

Idaho has a muley population of 270,000, and hunters annually harvest about 65,000 animals for a success rate of 30%. Idaho is also a top trophy state for mule deer and its 77 entries in the record book is second only to Colorado. I have a friend who lives along the Utah/Idaho border and he assures me that the new world record muley will be coming out of that area one of these days.

Montana

Montana has a population of about 350,000 mule deer, and hunters kill about 43,000 muleys annually with an impressive success rate of 48%. Montana also has 28 entries in the Boone & Crockett record book.

In addition, eastern Montana usually has several areas which offer multiple deer tags to keep down crop damage, and sportsmen find the combination of good deer numbers, big bucks, high success rates, plus multiple deer tags very attractive.

Oregon

Oregon has a mule deer population of about 300,000, and hunters harvest about 50,000 animals annually for a 31% success rate. Oregon also has 21 entries in the Boone & Crockett record book. State officials expect the mule deer herd to continue to grow and thereby improve a hunter's chances for success even more.

New Mexico

New Mexico hunters kill about 120,000 mule deer annually out of a herd of about 270,000 animals for a success rate of 22%. There are 53 entries from New Mexico in the record book. Even though some of New Mexico's statistics are not overly impressive, you have to be impressed with its trophy potential.

Arizona

Arizona hunters harvest about 12,000 mule deer annually from a herd of about 150,000 animals, for a success rate of 23%. But more importantly, Arizona has 52 entries in the Boone & Crockett record book. The deer throughout much of Arizona are scattered through rough, brushy terrain but there are some big trophy bucks to be had.

Washington

Washington has a stable mule deer herd of 140,000 and hunters annually kill about 26,000 mule deer for a success rate of 27 percent. Washington also claims 14 entries in the record book.

Nevada

Though Nevada is noted more as a desert state, there is still some excellent mule deer habitat in the mountains, which harbor a herd of about 130,000 and hunters every year kill about 11,000 animals for a success rate of 52%. While there are currently no Nevada entries in the Boone & Crockett record book, it looks like a hunter after mule deer in Nevada has better than a 50-50 chance to score.

BLACK BEAR

Idaho

Idaho is the best bear hunting state in the west. I know that from personal experience with bow and rifle. Hunters annually kill about 2,200 bears during the generous spring and fall bear seasons.

Idaho's rugged, brushy terrain is well suited for black bears, and there is ample grass for bruin in spring. The high country also produces large huckleberry crops in the mountains, and the bears gorge on this high calorie fruit in preparation for hibernation. Consequently, both adults and newborn cubs usually come out of hibernation in good shape.

Montana

Montana hunters kill about 1,700 black bears annually, mostly in the rugged western mountains where terrain and food supply matches that of Idaho. Montana also offers a spring and fall bear season.

Oregon

The lush rain fed forests along the Oregon coast furnish excellent bear habitat and hunters kill about 1,300 bears each year. In addition, hunters have a bonus in Oregon because they can kill one bear during the spring season and one during the fall season.

Washington

Washington's western forests are much like Oregon's, but Washington also has good bear hunting in the northeastern corner of the state. Hunters annually harvest about 1,200 bears.

Colorado

Colorado hunters kill about 650 bears during the spring and fall bear seasons, mostly in the foothills of the rugged northern mountains.

The best moose hunting in the West is found in Wyoming where hunters harvest about 1,500 animals annually.

All western states offer mountain lion hunting, but Utah has the largest annual harvest.

Wyoming

Wyoming is not a good bear state. There simply is not enough food for a large bear population. The fall berry crop that is so critical to a bear's winter survival is not there. Consequently, hunters kill only about 220 bears each year.

Arizona, New Mexico, Utah, Nevada

Arizona, New Mexico, and Utah are not considered good bear states, although there is a small, huntable bear population where the terrain will support them. Arizona harvests about 200 bears, New Mexico 200, and Utah 75. Nevada has no viable bear population.

ANTELOPE

Wyoming is by far the best state for antelope. It issues about 115,000 permits annually, which is more than all the other western states combined. Hunter success is also impressive, about 92%.

The vast sagebrush prairies of southeastern Wyoming support a huge herd of about 400,000 antelope. Officials often must go begging to get enough hunters to keep the herd trimmed. Consequently, multiple permits are offered in some areas.

Montana

Montana harvests about 35,000 antelope each year, mostly in the eastern half of the state. Hunter success is high, at about 90%. The state has allowed up to four antelope per hunter to be harvested in some eastern hunting districts to keep down crop damage.

Colorado

Colorado is a distant third in antelope harvest, at about 9,000. Hunter success is about 70%. Colorado is a marginal state for the nonresident who has his heart set on a nice buck antelope. With these lower antelope numbers, competition for a tag becomes increasingly stiff. There are usually far more applications than licenses issued.

Rest Of The West

The rest of the western states have very limited access to antelope hunting, and permits are difficult to obtain. Idaho is probably the best, with about 2,000 antelope harvested annually, and New Mexico is next with a harvest of about 1,700.

The hunter after a record book antelope would be wise to consider some of these states which offer limited access. The controlled hunting conditions often result in a disproportionate number of trophy sized bucks available. Arizona is a good example. The annual kill is only about 700, yet Arizona's 62 entries in the Boone & Crockett record book is second only to Wyoming.

MOOSE

Wyoming

Wyoming is tops for moose hunting in the west, with a population of about 9,000. Hunters kill about 1,500 moose every fall. Hunter success is about 80%, and 75% are bulls. Wyoming also is tops in the record book with 131 entries.

Wyoming issues moose permits, like all the other western states, on a drawing basis. If you plan to hunt any western state, apply for one of these limited permits. Every year many nonresident sportsmen receive a super bonus addition to their western dream hunt when they get drawn for one of these special hunts.

Bighorn sheep permits are tough to obtain, but Montana still allows unlimited sheep hunting in certain areas.

Montana & Idaho

Montana has a heathy moose population, and hunters kill about 400 animals every year. The southwestern part of the state is best for moose. Idaho is next, with about 225 moose harvested annually.

Rest Of The West

The other western states offer a very limited number of moose permits, and competition is difficult. Nevada has no viable moose population.

MOUNTAIN LION

All of the western states offer lion hunting. Some of the hunting is by permit drawing. A guide is a must, because of the specially trained hounds needed to run and tree a lion.

Utah has the highest lion harvest in the West, with a kill of about 220 lions annually, followed by Arizona with 200, Idaho with 190, Washington 170, Wyoming and Colorado 100 each, Montana 90, Oregon 60, and Nevada 50. California has the highest lion population, but does not allow nonresident lion hunting.

An attractive aspect of western lion hunting is that several states allow an unlimited number of permits. A guy who has his heart set on an exciting cougar hunt will have no problem in Arizona, Idaho, Montana, Nevada, New Mexico, Oregon, Utah, and Wyoming.

BIGHORN SHEEP

Bighorn sheep are scarce and very few permits are offered in western states. The exception is Montana. The Big Sky State still offers an unlimited bighorn sheep hunt in the rugged Madison Range north of Yellowstone National Park. When a quota has been reached in this area, the season is closed. This is a great place for the guy who has his heart set on a sheep hunt, but can't afford the money required to go up to Canada.

Idaho

Idaho also offers an unlimited sheep hunt in the rugged Salmon River Country. However, much of this area is so rough and remote that some hunting units have no sheep killed in them during an entire hunting season. However, other Idaho units are excellent hunting by permit drawing, and success is high in these areas. An annual kill of about 200 sheep is typical for Idaho.

Idaho also allows an unlimited sheep hunt in the remote Salmon River country.

Wyoming

Wyoming has a healthy sheep population, and hunting is allowed by permit drawing only. About 170 bighorns are harvested annually, and the success rate is about 40%.

Colorado

Colorado has a small, but stable bighorn sheep herd, and all hunting is done by permit drawing. About 50 bighorns are harvested annually, and success is high.

MOUNTAIN GOAT

Goat hunting is very limited in the western states. Washington is probably the best bet to try for a permit. It's also the best bet to try for the record book. Obviously, the goat habitat in Washington's mountain peaks is conducive to trophy-sized goats because 5 of the top 6 animals in the Boone & Crockett record book come from Washington, including the current world record.

Washington has the best mountain goat hunting. Currently, five of the top six goats in the record book come from this state.

WHITETAIL DEER

Most eastern hunters overlook whitetail deer hunting when planning a western hunt because they want to hunt new and exotic species. However, western whitetails are known for their trophy size, and any diehard whitetail hunter should look into the possibility of hunting for a trophy sized whitetail.

A few years back, I guided a Minnesota hunter on a trophy bull elk hunt. This guy was crazy about whitetails, and he was amazed by the sizes of some of the bucks he encountered. We finally took two days off from elk hunting and went after whitetails. He shot the largest whitetail buck of his hunting career, a big five-pointer (western count) with a 20-inch inside spread. Oh yes, he also got his bull elk.

The main reason why western whitetail bucks are so big is simply a matter of hunting pressure. The average age of a harvested eastern buck is only 1½ years, barely old enough to have forked antlers. On the other hand, the average age of a western whitetail is about 3⅓ years old, and plenty of big bucks die of old age.

Utah, Nevada, and California are the only western states that do not have whitetails. Arizona and New Mexico are also given over mostly to

Most eastern hunters overlook whitetails out West. However, trophy size whitetails can be found in many areas where hunting pressure is often nonexistent.

mule deer, except for a few isolated pockets of Coues' deer, a stunted subspecies of the whitetail deer family. All of the other western states have healthy whitetail populations, but western Montana and northern Idaho are best because those states have the brushy terrain that whitetails prefer.

GRIZZLY BEAR

Surprisingly, grizzly bear hunting is still allowed in the lower states. The state of Montana allows an annual kill quota of 25 grizzlies to be harvested to keep the population of this great bear from overflowing into areas where habitat is not ideal for its man-free existence.

Although the grizzly is still on the Endangered Species List, the bear has been doing so well in the Glacier and Yellowstone ecosystems that there is some talk of upgrading its status to something less critical than the "threatened" category. The good news for prospective grizzly bear hunters is that they don't have to rely on a million-to-one lottery to get a grizzly tag. Any hunter can obtain a grizzly tag, but the season is closed when the kill quota is reached. This is a great opportunity for the hunter who can't afford the exhorbitant prices for a grizzly hunt north of the border, but yearns for a chance to hunt this great bear. Currently, grizzly hunting is centered around the Bob Marshall Wilderness area south of Glacier National Park.

Deep snowfall locks motorized traffic out of much of the high country, making it excellent security areas for wildlife and better hunting areas for hunters willing to pay the physical price of getting into it.

Chapter 3

PLANNING A GUIDED HUNT

Two factors influence a hunter's decision to make a guided hunt. First, he must greatly desire to return from his dream hunt with a trophy. Second, he must be able to afford to pay for the privilege of a guided hunt.

There is another reason why a sportsman might choose to hire a guide — comfort. John Macaluso of Murrysville, Pennsylvania, said it well when he told me, "I work hard all year to be able to afford to go elk hunting, and I don't want to worry about making supper in the rain, or moving camp, or packing out game. My hunting is for my pleasure, and it's nice to have a guide to take care of all that stuff."

Without a doubt, the hunter with a guide stands a much better chance for success. Take elk hunting as an example. The average success rate for unguided elk hunters is about 15%, while the success rate for guided hunters is about 36%.

A good guide furnishes two vital requirements for any western hunt. He knows the land, and he knows the habits of the game. He combines this knowledge into a plan that should ultimately bring the hunter into position to bring down his trophy.

It's not too difficult to decide to make a guided hunt, but it's a whole different matter when it comes to actually choosing the stranger whom you will entrust to help make your dream hunt a success. There are many horror stories about clients who paid a lot of money to some shady outfitter, but received very little help once in camp.

While it is true that there are some questionable outfitters still in operation, there are many more who are honest and try very hard to furnish everything to a client that was agreed upon. In fact, all of the western states put strict controls on their outfitters.

An outfitter must first pass a state test before he can advertise, and he must also provide a performance and insurance bond before he can ac-

Some hunters choose to a guided hunt to avoid the chore of setting up camp and packing out game.

tually take clients on a hunt. In addition, an outfitter must keep meticulous records of his operations and then hand them in to the state at the end of hunting season. Any complaints about an outfitter are taken seriously and investigated by state officials.

There are four basic types of hunts that an outfitter may offer a client. They are the bare bones, drop camp, standard hunt, and trophy hunt. They not only vary greatly in price, but they also vary greatly in their potential for success. Before a hunter begins his search for an outfitter, he should have some idea of the type of hunt he wants to make.

Bare Bones

The bare bones hunt usually consists of an outfitter putting up a client in his main hunting lodge or camp and providing room and board, but nothing else. The hunter is on his own to go out and find the game. He also must field dress any game he kills, and he almost always has to pay the outfitter to have his game packed back to camp.

This is a good hunt for someone who wants to experience the excitement of western big game hunting in a rustic camp setting, but would not be heartbroken if he returned home without a trophy. A bare bones hunt is a good way to get accustomed to western hunting at a leisurely pace, and some hunters use this type of hunt as a stepping stone to a self guided hunt.

The bare bones hunt varies greatly between outfitters. Some outfitters are nice enough to take each client out for a short tour of the area to point out how and where to hunt nearby game. Other outfitters have no time for these low-paying clients and furnish nothing more than room and board in a woodsy setting. If you plan to take a bare bones hunt, get the outfitter to commit himself to show you a few decent hunting spots near camp.

The advantage of a bare bones hunt is the low cost. Sure it might cost $100 per day, but that's not much more than the cost of a hunter staying in a motel and eating in restaurants. In addition, most hunting camps are exciting places to be during hunting season, and many clients return every year just to be around the campfire during hunting season.

The disadvantage of a bare bones hunt is that hunter success is low. There are also several hidden costs that can be incurred during this hunt, such as packing, transportation, laundry, etc.

Drop Camp

A drop camp is so named because an outfitter takes the clients into a prearranged area where he has set up a completely self-contained camp and then drops them off to hunt on their own. The camp is usually situated in a backcountry area where there is ample game nearby, and hunting is good.

The outfitter normally has a guide visit the drop camp every three days to assist the hunters with any problems they might have, or to pack out game. Other than that, the hunters are on their own. They must cook their own meals and find their own game during a drop camp hunt. Consequently, they still must have some understanding of where to find a particular species of game and how to hunt it.

A drop camp is attractive to hunters who want some help in getting into a promising hunting area, but would like to hunt on their own. Bowhunters after elk especially like this type of hunt because they can easily locate bugling bulls.

Even rifle hunters can have a good hunt from a drop camp. I know of two gun hunters from Minnesota who had to talk an outfitter into taking them into a drop camp. The men couldn't afford full guiding fees, and the outfitter normally did not offer drop camp hunting. Before the outfitter left, he even apologized for the poor hunting area he had to leave them in. But the surprise was on him because both men killed elk from that drop camp, and one of the bulls was a huge 6-point.

There are also a few horror stories associated with drop camps. One group of hunters got lucky and killed two deer and a spike bull elk on their

There are four basic types of outfitted hunts: bare bones, drop camp, standard hunt, and trophy hunt.

first day hunting, but the guide did not show up to pack out the meat for four days, and it had soured by then.

A friend of mine told me that he was in a drop camp a few years ago where the food was so meager and unappetizing that the guys had to spend time hunting grouse to keep from starving! The guide showed little sympathy for their plight, and he never did bring in adequate provisions on his two return trips.

A drop camp hunt can be an excellent way to make your dream hunt in the west, but a hunter should be very careful to get in writing all the services that will be provided on a drop camp. There are too many variables in this type of hunt that can ruin it if not taken care of.

The advantage of a drop camp hunt is its moderate cost, usually around $150 per day per hunter (with a minimum of three hunters). Hunters are taken in to a remote area where the game lives, and they don't have to bother with setting up a camp or horses.

The disadvantage of a drop camp is the lack of guiding expertise. The hunters still must be knowledgeable in the habitat and habits of the game they are hunting. They must do all their own cooking, plus camp chores. They also must field dress and properly hang any game they kill. There may be added hidden expenses such as cost of food or a packing fee.

Standard Guided Hunt

The standard guided hunt is the one most taken by hunters who hire an outfitter. Standard procedure on this type of hunt is to have one guide for every two hunters. The biggest attraction here is the expertise of a guide who has a thorough knowledge of the land and the game. This expertise is the commodity that a client is mostly paying for.

Guide expertise is also an asset that is difficult to put a price tag on. You are paying a man for what he knows, but you really don't have any idea if he is an expert woodsman or just some unemployed local resident. And the longer a client goes without seeing game, the more he tends to become suspicious of his guide's worth.

Sometimes a client has a legitimate gripe about a guide when it becomes obvious that the man is not an expert woodsman. On the other hand, there will be times when even a good guide will not be able to get his client into position for a shot at a trophy. I had one client on an elk rifle hunt in Montana who was an enjoyable man to be around. He was willing to work hard right alongside me, and I thought he fully understood when several promising hunts did not turn out. In return, I worked very hard to help him take him a trophy. You can imagine my disappointment when he informed me upon his departure that he felt he had "wasted" his money because I did not get him an elk.

The advantage of the standard guided hunt is the invaluable hunting expertise of a guide. A client usually has his lodging, food, and transportation furnished, and an outfitter will do all the field dressing and packing.

The disadvantage of a standard guided hunt is the high cost. Also, there is the difficulty of having two hunters for one guide. If only one trophy is spotted during the course of the hunt, and it's not your turn to shoot that day, you will go home empty-handed.

Trophy Hunt

A guided trophy hunt is for the client who has a specific trophy requirement during his hunt. A common requirement on an elk trophy hunt is a six-point bull. I've even had a client tell me that he wanted a six-point bull that scored at least 350 points.

A guided trophy hunt usually requires a client to have his own guide, and his man must be a top hand. This hunt is often very strenuous and sometimes less exciting because a guide must often take his client into rugged backcountry where the trophy animals are more likely to be found.

I had one client who I was personally guiding on a trophy hunt for a big six-point bull elk. We had several very tough hunts with no luck, and this man became increasingly disgruntled because the other clients who were on a standard guided hunt seemed to always be into elk. I explained that we had to get back away from the herds of cows and spike bulls to where

The advantage of a bare bones hunt is its low cost. Success on a bare bone elk hunt is usually low, but hunters often do well on deer.

the big bachelor bulls were hiding. The man did not get his trophy bull, and he left camp feeling that he had been shortchanged.

The advantage of a trophy guided hunt is that a client has his own personal guide throughout his hunt, and this guide is usually one of the most experienced men who can seek out the hiding places of the trophy animals.

The disadvantage of this hunt is the cost, usually around $3,000 for a seven day hunt. In addition, this may actually be a more strenuous hunt during which less game is seen.

The Search For An Outfitter

The search for a good outfitter who will serve your needs is a difficult task and requires a lot of homework. The best place to begin your search is in the advertisements in the back of outdoor magazines. You can read these ads to get a general idea of what a particular outfitter offers, but never call one up and book a hunt soley on his ad campaign and personality over the phone. That's a good way to end up with a less than fruitful hunt.

I had an experience several years ago with an outfitter in Idaho that typifies the problems that a hasty decision can create. I'd met this outfitter while scouting for game, and the man not only had a very outgoing personality, but the hunting success that he claimed was amazing. He quoted an overall success rate of 80% on elk, 70% on deer, and 50% on bear.

I'm always getting phone calls and letters from sportsmen across the country asking for a good area to hunt or a competent guide to hire. I told three men about this outfitter, and I suggested they give him a try.

A year later I discovered that his success claim was a lie, that the Forest Service was taking away his hunting area, and the state was revoking his outfitter's license. The man was unlawful, and unethical. He got put out of business, but not before he ruined many a hunt for anyone unfortunate enough to have booked with him.

My point is that any outfitter can make inaccurate claims for success and talk a good game over the phone. A hunter planning his western dream hunt must be careful and proceed cautiously to make sure that an outfitter is both honest and hard working.

That's not to say that most outfitters are shady characters. Quite the contrary. Outfitters as a whole are hard working businessmen who try their best to give a client what he paid for. I personally know more than 20 outfitters in Idaho and Montana, and none of them would ever try to misrepresent himself.

The best way to initiate contact with an outfitter is in writing. When you find an outfitter who interests you, write a letter describing the hunt that you would like to make, and ask him if he could furnish such a hunt. Request his rates and enclose a list of questions covering such areas as the

A drop camp is attractive to many hunters because of its moderate cost. In addition, a camp already set up in the backcountry greatly improves the chances of success.

type of terrain he hunts in, his hunter success rates, references, guide-to-hunter ratio, etc.

Questions To Ask An Outfitter

1. What type of terrain is the hunting done in? (Is it steep and brushy, or gentle with open parks, etc.)   2. How is his operation run? (Try to determine if he seems too disorganized.)

3. How many hunters does he run through his camp weekly and annually? (A large number of clients each week might mean that you will not receive personal attention.)

4. How many hunters per guide? (The standard is two hunters per guide.)

5. Will there be any additional expenses? (For transportation to and from airport, packaging and shipping meat, etc.)

6. What are the primary big game animals in the area, and what extra game might be hunted from permit drawings?) The main animals might be elk and deer, but a guy who draws a permit might also be able to hunt more exotic game such as sheep or goats.)

7. What is the success rate? (Ask for a breakdown — six mule deer

The standard guided hunt is the one most taken by hunters who hire an outfitter.

were killed out of 12 hunters for a 50% success ratio for deer.

8. What is the best time during the season to hunt the particular game species that you are interested in? (Find out if those prime time slots have been filled already.)

9. What possible price variations can be made to accommodate the type of hunt you are interested in? (This is the time when you should detail the type of hunt you want — drop camp, standard hunt, etc.)

10. What kind of deposit will be required? (This varies, but most outfitters require a 50% deposit before a booking is confirmed.)

If you like what you read in his reply, follow that up with a phone call to get a better feel for the type of man you're dealing with. Ask more questions that might have popped into your mind. Repeat this entire procedure with several promising outfitters until you are certain that you have the outfitter who is best for you.

Success Rates

Success rates can be misleading. An ad that I read recently offering deer and elk hunts claimed an 80% success rate. I knew that this par-

A guided trophy hunt is for the client who has a specific trophy requirement, such as this mature bull elk.

Success rates among outfitters can be misleading. Make sure the success rate you are quoted is for the species of game you are interested in.

ticular outfitter had nowhere near that type of success. When I asked him, he explained that only 20% of his clients actually killed elk, but there were so many young muley bucks in the area that just about every client killed one. Consequently, his claim of 80% success overall for both deer and elk was misleading for the hunter who was primarily after elk.

References

References can be another misleading area when searching for an outfitter. Even the poorest outfitter will occassionally get lucky and one of his clients will kill something. If you ask that outfitter for three references, he may send you the names of the only three guys who killed any game with him in the past three years!

Always ask for about six references, and don't be afraid to ask for a few names of clients who did not kill game the past year. If a client went home empty-handed, but will still recommend an outfitter, you can be sure that he must have worked hard for his client, and the client recognized and appreciated it.

Bowhunters in particular must be diligent when searching for a competent outfitter. An archer needs a guide who understands the limitations of a bow and can bring the game in, or get the client in close enough for a shot. An outfitter may have a 50% success rate overall on trophy sized muley bucks, but if none of his clients have yet to kill a big buck with bow and arrow, you had better keep looking.

Elk bowhunters also have problems with outfitters. This is because most guides do not have the expertise to bugle in a rutting bull elk to bow range. I would suggest that an archer book only with an outfitter who is himself an elk bowhunter. Some guides eventually catch on to the special needs of the archery hunter and do well, even though they are not bowhunters themselves. This type of nonbowhunting guide who has successfully guided archers in the past could also be acceptable.

What To Expect From Your Outfitter

A client should expect integrity from his outfitter, and all services agreed to by contract should be fulfilled. In addition, an outfitter should furnish his client with a competent guide who has a good understanding of the game and its habitats and tries hard to get the client a trophy. The guide should also know the land and have more than one plan of action in case a particular hunt does not pan out due to weather, etc.

A client should expect his guide to work hard to get him within range of the game.

A good guide should also be capable of field dressing and caping out a trophy in the field. Meat should be carefully handled and packed out to a decent storage facility.

The above is just about all a client can realistically expect from an outfitter. Things such as comradery, intelligent conversation, and companionship after hours are all nice additions, but not all men are capable or interested in the social graces. Hope for the best with your guide's personality, but remember, you are paying soley for his expertise in the field.

What An Outfitter Expects From His Client

An outfitter expects his clients to show up in reasonably good physical condition. I have had several clients lose chances at trophy sized bull elk because they could not sustain a brisk pace uphill for five minutes. It is difficult for me to understand a man spending thousands of dollars for his western dream hunt, and then not working out to toughen up his body.

Some clients are also under the impression that they don't need to get into shape because most of the hunting will be from horses. Horses are used mostly to get the hunter into the backcountry. The hunting is still usually on foot. It is not unusual to travel on horseback three miles in to a remote area at first light and then hunt hard on foot for the rest of the day through rough terrain where the animals are holed up.

An outfitter also expects his client to be able to make a killing shot at reasonable range. I would call a 300 yard shot at a mule deer a reasonable shot with a steady hold for the rifle. My guiding partner Jim Monzie told me about a client who missed two big muley bucks and a dandy bull elk, all under 300 yards. The guy then had the nerve to tell the outfitter that Jim had not done his job because the guy was going home empty-handed!

That leads to another point. An outfitter's job is to get a client into position for a killing shot, which may be upwards to 400 yards. The outfitter has done his job. He can coach and help a client to make a good shot, but the end result, be it hit or miss, rests with the client.

When I outfitted, I tried very hard to get my client into reasonable range. I'd watch the client ready for the shot, and I always felt that my job as a guide was complete. It was up to him whether he hit or missed. I've never felt guilty about a client going home empty-handed if I gave him at least one reasonable shot at the game.

Taking time to carefully glass out the upper end of a basin like this is critical to elk hunting success in the Rockies.

Chapter 4

PLANNING A SELF-GUIDED HUNT

Sportsmen choose to make a self-guided western hunt for one of two reasons. They either can't afford the cost of a guided hunt, or they want to do things their own way.

Sportsmen who dream of making a western big game hunt come from all walks in life, and not all these men can afford the cost of a guided hunt. It's tough enough for them to come up with the $1,200 for a self-guided hunt, but the $3,000 needed for a guided hunt is economically out of the question.

Surprisingly, there are men who have the resources to make a guided hunt, but they'd rather do it themselves. I've met a lot of them, and they are the do-it-yourself type of individuals who get as much enjoyment out of the year-long planning as they do from the hunt.

Besides being more economical, a self-guided hunt can provide a lot of self-satisfaction to a sportsman. In fact, some of the digging and planning done long before the hunt can be as challenging, rewarding, and just plain enjoyable as the taking of the trophy that you will bring home when everything comes together during the hunt.

Research Is The Key

Nonresident sportsmen from all over the country who make successful western hunts on their own every year have a common warning to others who would like to do the same: "If you want to make a self-guided hunt in the West, you'd better do your homework." They also point out the need for intense research to find the the most productive hunting areas. I don't mean a generality, such as northern Wyoming for elk; I'm talking about specifics such as a particular mountainside in northern Wyoming where big bull elk can be found, or a certain drainage where the four-point

The self-guided hunter must do his homework if he wants his hunt to be a success.

muleys are sure to be found.

Ed Palley of West Trenton, New Jersey, hunts almost every year in either Colorado or Wyoming for elk, and he cautions would-be hunters to begin making phone calls a year before the actual hunt begins. Ed told me, "I do a lot of phoning to state wildlife agencies, local hunting clubs, and friends of friends. I make sure that there are plenty of elk in an area before I make plans to hunt there. Another thing I do during my research is to make requests from states for their previous year's elk kill county-by-county, and even drainage-by-drainage if I can get it. That tells me quickly where the elk are being killed in a state."

Is there any wonder why Ed Pallay is a successful unguided elk hunter? Ed is typical of the many unguided hunters who use a variety of methods to run down hunting leads until they have exhausted every means of gaining further information on a hunting area located some 3,000 miles from home. It's the only way to insure the best possible chance for success on a western big game hunt.

Sources of Where-To-Go Information

Appendix A

Appendix A is located in the back of this book right after Chapter 10. There has never been a more complete listing of where-to-go information compiled to aid the nonresident hunter in his search for a good area to hunt in the western states. This appendix lists, by species, the known productive hunting areas in each western state. In addition, the appendix also notes the areas which have the greatest trophy potential.

This information is both vital and accurate. It is the result of an exhaustive research effort by the author to provide a good starting point for a hunter who wants to make a western hunt. It's not theoretical guesswork idly picked off topographical maps; it's actual hunting areas recommended by some of the most knowledgeable big game hunters in the west. Pick one of these areas and start making phone calls!

Magazine Articles

Magazine articles are an excellent source of information to begin your search for a good hunting area. Outdoor magazine editors in recent years have demanded more information on "where-to-go" hunts, and the result is a good starting place for the hunter looking for a decent area to hunt a particular species of game.

Unfortunately for the nonresident, most major magazines now operate on a regional format, and a guy who lives in Florida may not have access to the western regional edition of magazines such as *Outdoor Life* or *Field & Stream*, which routinely publish western where-to-go articles. If

Appendix A in the back of this book will point out areas in the West to find trophy mule deer such as this buck.

that is the case, use Appendix A.

One note of warning. A writer in an outdoor magazine is usually detailing an exciting hunt that he had in an area, and it often reads like the entire country is overpopulated with huge black bears or antelope with 16-inch horns. Remember that any area where a hunt is successful will sound like a great spot to hunt. The truth of the matter is that every outdoor article written about a particular area may not be the very best place to hunt where the chance for success is greatest. Sure you can use the article for the focus of your research, but go on with more intense information.

Big Game Statistics

You've heard the saying, "Numbers don't lie." Well, when it comes to hunting statistics, the numbers can often be a lot more truthful than the advice of a stranger over the phone. Every western state keeps statistics of big game kills for each hunting unit in that state. In addition, they sometimes keep track of other things that could help, such as the amount of hunters who use an area, or the number of hunter hours afield per kill. These statistics not only tell you where the animals are being harvested,

Talk to other hunters who have made western hunts. Oftentimes, they can point out excellent areas where bull elk like this one can be located.

but also how many hunters use the area and how hard they have to hunt to kill their game.

The best way to receive statistical information from a western state is to enclose a self-addressed, stamped return envelope (SASE) to make their job easier. I once requested information from 16 states, and I included an SASE with 10 of the letters. I got back a reply from all of the states in which I'd enclosed an SASE, but only two of the states that did not have an SASE enclosed bother to send a reply.

Another tip is to request statistics for the hunting period two years back. If you request information for the previous year, chances are that the state will reply that their statistics have not yet been compiled for the previous year. Besides, you want general information on where the game is being taken, and harvests do not change much from year to year in the prime hunting areas.

State Wildlife Agencies

Every western state has several wildlife agencies located in various regions of the state. Once you have located a promising area, call the wildlife office in that area and ask to talk to a wildlife biologist. These men are very helpful, and you will almost always hang up the phone with a whole lot more information than you'd hoped for.

While you are talking to the wildlife biologist, ask for any names of local sportsmen, sporting goods stores, or clubs that might be of help. Follow up any leads in this area with another phone call.

Acquaintances

Talk to men who have made hunts similar to the one you plan to go on. I met a man from Kentucky a few years ago while bowhunting in northern Idaho. Even though this was his first western hunt, the guy had just killed a four-point bull elk, and I asked him how he'd discovered such a good elk archery area.

The guy told me that when he decided to hunt elk with a bow, he started asking around about anyone who had made a western big game hunt in recent years. He came up with the friend of a friend of a friend who had rifle hunted in Idaho and he called this man, hoping for some little bit of information.

The stranger on the other end of the phone call praised the area of north Idaho where he'd rifle hunted and assured the bowhunter that archery hunting also would be excellent. A follow-up phone call to a state wildlife biologist in northern Idaho confirmed the area's elk hunting potential, and the successful hunt was planned from one simple phone call to a stranger.

Making contact with acquaintances is an open area for a prospective western big game hunter, and much of the fruit of this labor depends on how hard a guy works at it. I've even heard of some hunters who used their membership in national clubs such as the NRA or Elks club to bring them in contact with members who could help them find a good hunting area.

Trophy Hunting Problems

Trophy hunting on a self-guided hunt is difficult. The record book animals are never plentiful in any area, and the hunters who try a self-guided hunt are at a distinct disadvantage. It's hard enough for the distant nonresident to locate a suitable hunting area, let alone locate a spot where the big trophy sized animals roam.

Another factor which limits trophy hunting on a self-guided hunt is the time element. The average seven day hunt is simply not long enough for a hunter to pass up decent animals in the hope that he'll kill a record book specimen before he leaves.

Probably the best way to make your hunt have the most trophy potential is to try extra hard to hunt in an area known for its record-book sized game animals. The record book is the quickest source of information to find out which state provides the best trophy potential for the big game

The self-guided hunter should know what type of terrain the animals will be found in. A topographical map will also help because it shows you what to expect from the land before you get there.

Trophy hunting is a problem for the self-guided hunter. Most trophy animals are found in secluded backcountry areas.

that you plan to hunt. In addition, Appendix A points out the best trophy producing areas of each western state.

Learning About Big Game Habits And Habitat

A guided hunter doesn't really have to know anything about the big game he plans to hunt. After all, that's what he pays the guide for. However, the hunter on a self-guided hunt must know all the important facts about the big game animals which he will hunt.

The self-guided hunter should know what type of habitat the animals prefer, their daily feeding and bedding habits, and their tendencies when hunted. I remember stopping at a camp a few years back in Idaho where three dejected bowhunters were huddled around a fire. I'd just had a terrific hunt about seven miles from their camp in which I'd come very close to killing a bugling bull elk.

The men told me that they were from Georgia, and they had been hunting hard for five days without seeing an elk. As I listened further, it became apparent that they had picked an excellent drainage to hunt elk, but they had no idea of how to hunt them. Their daily hunting routine was to slowly spread out from camp (located next to a major logging road!) and still-hunt like they did for whitetails back home. You can imagine their shock that evening when I took them up to the wild high country where they heard their first elk bugle.

The best way to learn about the habits of big game that interests you is to take advantage of the many excellent outdoor books written by hunting and wildlife experts. In recent years, several in-depth books which explore both the daily habits and hunting techniques of western big game have been offered commercially that greatly improve the chances of hunting success for any reader who is seriously planning a western hunting trip. Another excellent source of information is videos. And in some ways, western hunting videos are even more valuable than books. For example, a video on Rocky Mountain mule deer not only explains the habits and habitat where muleys live, but it also "shows" you through exciting hunting action scenes what it's like to hunt an animal such as mule deer.

Bowhunters who intend to go after rutting bull elk would be smart to purchase a cassette instructional elk bugling tape to learn how to simulate a bull's bugle. It always amazes me how proficient some nonresidents can get with an elk bugle after practicing with one of these tapes.

I invited three Wisconsin hunters to join me for an elk bowhunt in Montana four years ago, and I suggested that they practice their bugling with an instructional tape. I hoped that they'd be marginally acceptable at bugling by the time they arrived, but the surprise was on me. They were great! In fact, one of them sounded better than I ever did. Oh yes, as a reward for their diligence, they got to take home a cow and two bulls, one of which was a dandy Pope & Young trophy which scored 300 points.

Access To Your Hunting Area

The method of access to a good hunting area is often overlooked by hunters who are unfamiliar with rugged western terrain. It's also an oversight that can turn a dream trip into a nightmare.

You may find a red hot hunting area, but if you can't come up with a reasonable plan to get into it, you'd better keep looking. The Bob Marshall Wilderness area in western Montana is a good example. Everyone knows that it's tops for elk hunting, but not everyone knows that the "tops" elk hunting is in the backcountry, requiring a hike of about seven miles in some areas. And I don't mean a gentle footpath, I mean steep, rugged trails that tax even the most sure-footed hikers.

Once you find a good hunting spot, decide how you will gain access. Keep in mind that nonresidents find the rugged western terrain very difficult for hiking. A mile in Minnesota is far different from a mile in the Wind River country of Colorado. And for most nonresidents who are unaccustomed to the high altitude and steep terrain, a hunting area farther than two miles from a road should be avoided.

Horses are the obvious answer to gain access to those backcountry hotspots, and every year I see sportsmen from as far away as Texas, or

Oklahoma, or California bringing horses into the rugged Bitterroot Mountains of western Montana. I've even had a few nonresident western hunting addicts tell me that they bought horses just to use on their western elk hunts.

An obvious question arises. If I don't have horses, will I be passing up all the prime hunting ground in the west? The answer is no. There is some good hunting to be found within a mile of busy four lane freeways. I know that for a fact. Most of my favorite elk hunting areas in Idaho and Montana are located within a mile of where I park my pickup.

Access is one item that you should bring up while you are talking to wildlife biologists and other western contacts while searching for a good hunting area. Always ask how difficult access is to a particular area, and ask how high in elevation you must climb to get there. There are some mountains in the Teton Range of northern Wyoming that are a mile up for every mile in, literally!

Topographical Maps Are Vital

Topographical maps are critical to the success of any unguided western big game hunt, and it doesn't matter whether you are hunting bull elk or antelope. A topo map will show you what to expect from the land before

Two excellent sources of information about how and where to hunt western game are videos and books.

The bowhunter who intends to hunt rutting bull elk would be smart to purchase an instructional elk bugling tape.

you ever lay eyes on it.

Appendix B lists all the sources of topo maps, and you should order all the maps from the small scale (half inch to the mile) national forest maps, to the large scale (4 inches to the mile) geological survey maps.

Those large scale topo maps are indispensable to an expert western big game hunter like Dwight Schuh. Dwight can take one quick look at a topo map and see how steep the terrain is, where the trails and roads are located, and he can even pick out the most promising hunting areas.

Once you learn more about the tendencies of the game that you will be hunting, you will be able to find good specific prime hunting spots from a topo map. For instance, from your research into the habits of antelope, you will know that water holes in typical arid antelope country are prime hunting spots, and you can quickly locate them from a topo map. You will also know that elk like the high country just below timberline, and especially the lush feeding areas around backcountry lakes. The topo map shows the timberline fringe and lakes, and you will already have a few "prime" hunting spots picked out for your dream hunt months before the trip.

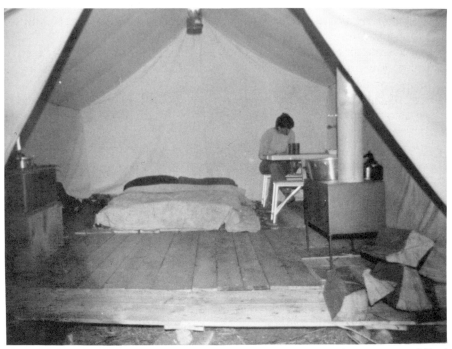

A backcountry camp is one way to enjoy hunting remote areas where access is difficult.

Chapter 5

PHYSICAL CONDITIONING

Every piece of advice written on western hunting stresses conditioning, yet every year outfitters are tortured by hunters who greatly desire to kill the trophy of a lifetime, but can't hike 200 feet uphill without gasping for breath. I believe that much of this problem is caused by a nonresident's lack of proper training and his inability to comprehend the rugged nature of hunting in some areas of the Rocky Mountains.

Wisconsin resident Jim Kimberly can tell you all about the physical conditioning you need on a western big game hunt. I'd guided Jim on a bowhunt for bull elk in western Montana several years ago. Jim's hunt was successful; he killed a dandy 6X7 bull that made the record book.

Jim also paid a high price physically, judging from the torrents of sweat that cascaded down his red face, because our hunt was very strenuous. But then, Jim got exactly what he wanted. He was adamant when he told me at the start of the hunt, "I'm in top shape. I'm willing to do anything and go anywhere with you to get a bull. I can keep up. Let's go for it!" We did, and he couldn't.

By the time Jim killed his bull, he'd been pushed to the limit of his physical capability and beyond. We were hunting steep, rugged country along the Idaho/Montana border. Jim kept up fairly well the first day, but after that, his legs could not recover from the shock of climbing those steep slopes.

It was discouraging for Jim because instead of getting better, he actually got worse. Slopes that he managed the first day were harder on him the third day. Jim killed his bull on the fifth day of his hunt after a punishing mile long "forced march" straight up a steep mountainside, which took more than an hour. In fact, the ground was so steep that we'd sometimes have to grab brush or clumps of grass to keep from sliding backward.

Jim told me after his hunt was over, "I was shocked how tough it was. I paid a lot of attention to conditioning before my hunt, and I read up on the geography of the area, but I wasn't prepared for the never-ending steepness of the high country. I realize now that I was doing health club exercises when I should have been working out with elk hunting in mind."

How tough was Jim Kimberly's elk bowhunt? My diary log notes that we hiked six miles the first day, seven miles the second day, nine miles the third day, and eight miles the fourth day. We'd hiked five miles on the fifth day before Jim killed his bull. And none of it was on level ground.

Many nonresident hunters experience the same problems that Jim Kimberly had. Jim had worked out and expected the hunt to be tough, but the sheer size and steepness of the western Rocky Mountains took him by surprise.

Jim Monzie guides for an outfitter in Montana and he knows all about the physical limits of a client. Jim told me, "I have a half dozen clients miss chances to kill elk and deer every year because they're not in shape.

"I had one guy with me last year when we kicked a big herd of elk from a fir thicket. I could see that they were going to pass through a large opening to our left, and all we had to do was get up on a small ridge and we'd have our pick of them. The ridge was only 300 feet above us, but we had

Physical conditioning is vital for the hunter who wants to get back to the high country after a bull elk like this one.

to hurry. The guy just didn't have the push to get there quickly. He had to stop and rest twice.

"I hurried ahead of him to locate the biggest bull and be ready to point it out when the hunter got there. There must have been 30 elk that walked across that clearing, and there were two nice bulls that I could see. I waited and waited. Finally the bulls were at the end of the clearing when I looked back to urge the guy on. He was standing 30 feet below me resting! He didn't even believe me that the clearing had been full of elk a minute before!"

Maybe if I tell enough horror stories about conditioning, enough prospective nonresident hunters will realize the seriousness of getting into shape. It's not just for comfort during the hunt. The lack of physical conditioning is directly proportional to the lack of success on many hunts.

Of course, if you are just after antelope, you could manage to hike along the rolling prairie even if you weren't in top shape. But for virtually all other big game, you have to be capable of hiking in steep, rugged terrain. It's almost criminal to spend all that time and money planning for your dream hunt, and then come out west soft.

Horse Hunting

Outfitter Harvey Mead related a conversation to me that he'd had with a client who was interested in booking an elk hunt. The man was adamant about not being interested in doing a lot of hiking, and since Harvey had horses, the man was certain that he would be able to do all his serious elk hunting from a saddle.

Harvey told him, "We'll use horses to get into the backcountry, but then we'll have to hunt the elk on foot."

The man scoffed and said, "I know horses! A horse can go anywhere that an elk can."

Harvey replied, "That's true, but you won't be on it when it does!"

Elk walk through open meadows and use trails when they are not hunted, but when they get pressured, they head for thickets and blowdown sanctuaries, and an outfitter will not even attempt to take a horse and rider into one. For one, it's too dangerous for the horse; and two, it's dangerous for the rider. It's also a poor way to hunt elk. If you are planning a guided western hunt, don't assume that you only have to ride a horse until an elk is spotted and then shoot it. There is still a lot of rough hiking involved in horse hunting, so you'd better prepare physically for it.

Getting Into Shape

A health club routine is excellent for body tone, and I would recommend it for anyone planning a western hunt in rugged country. However, the body parts that need the conditioning the most require specialized

Jogging is one of the best exercises to improve breathing and heart pulse rate.

workouts that closely approximate hunting conditions.

Two things hurt the average nonresident hunter out west — altitude and ground steepness. Altitude is a problem area that most hunters overlook when conditioning for a western hunt. Here's a typical situation. A guy from New York City is planning to hunt elk in the Wind River country of Colorado. The elevation of New York City is 100 feet above sea level, while the good elk country in Colorado is found somewhere around 8,000 feet. The air is much thinner at that elevation, and the guy who has not improved his breathing regularity will feel like he's run into an invisible wall when he starts hiking up one of those seemingly endless Rocky Mountains.

Obviously, there's not much that a man in the lowlands can do to perfectly simulate those high altitude conditions, but there are some things that he can do to improve his understanding of thin air exertion. Mount Marcy in the nearby Adirondack Mountains is only a two hour drive from New York City, and it is the highest peak in New York.

Mount Marcy is also readily accessible by trail to the top. If the guy from New York City was smart, he'd take a couple of hikes up to that high elevation during the summer before his trip to improve both his leg strength and wind. The feeling of lightheadedness he gets at that high elevation will help him recognize and be prepared for the limitations that the Colorado high country will put on him.

Jogging

Jogging is one of the best exercises to improve the intake capacity of your lungs. It also allows the body to perform more strenuous exercises without heavy breathing. If you don't normally jog, don't start trying to run 10 miles every day. Instead, begin with a light 2 mile run. After a week, add another mile until you are up to 10 miles. You'll be amazed how much jogging will improve not only your wind, but also your overall body tone.

Hiking

Hiking is the exercise that best simulates western hunting conditions. The problem arises when a guy doesn't live in a state that has any steep hills to hike up to simulate western terrain. My friend Bob Mussey of Wisconsin told me that there is virtually no mountainous terrain near his home to hike up.

Bob solved this problem by climbing stairs until his jelly-soft thighs and calves began to firm up. Then he put on a pack and progressively added weight to it to further push his leg muscles. It must have worked because I was genuinely impressed by Bob's ability to conquer the steep Bitterroot Mountains of northern Idaho.

Bicycling

Bicycling is an overlooked exercise for getting your legs into shape. I have guided three men who used bike riding to strengthen their legs, and I was impressed with the drive and power that their calves and thighs still had after an hour of hiking uphill.

One client told me that he worked at a plant in a city, and he didn't have a lot of time after work to exercise on his bike. He began riding his bike to work to build up his muscles. In the end he not only built up his muscles for his western hunt, but he also found a far more enjoyable method of maneuvering through the murderous traffic jams in the city.

Packing Out Game
(Subtitle: The Agony Without The Ecstasy!)

Packing out game, or drudgery as some of us experienced western hunters would be prone to call it, can quickly take the fun out of a hunt. Even a western woodsman in top shape will end up gasping for breath and muttering about the stupidity of western hunting after a trip or two of packing out 100 pound elk quarters from a steep draw far below an access road.

The self-guided nonresident who still doesn't have his western legs underneath him yet will be submitted to a torturous experience. Think

Hiking is the exercise that best simulates western hunting. Note that this man is strengthening his legs by hiking uphill with a weighted pack. He is also wearing the boots which he'll use during his hunt.

about the typical packing scenerio. A big bull elk is killed in a blowdown creek bottom two miles from the nearest access road. It's a 3,000 foot climb in elevation up to the road over rock outcrops and heavy blown down trees. Oh yes, to add a little spice to the situation, it's raining heavily.

If two men are hunting together, they will have to make two packs in and out of there to bring out all the meat plus antlers. I know of several instances where nonresidents attempted this type of pack, but had to give up after a short time because it was just too much for them. They ended up looking for a packer, but packers are in short supply in the middle of hunting season. And you can be sure that they paid dearly for their meat to be packed out.

The point here is that nonresidents, for that matter all of us, have some real physical limitations when it comes to certain areas of western big game hunting, and the elk is one of them. They are huge animals who inhabit steep, rugged terrain, and it is not unusual to have to pack out up to 400 pounds of meat, cape, hide, and antlers as a "reward" for a successful hunt.

I roam the rugged western high country all the time, and I'm not afraid to admit that I have limitations in this department. Due to creeping age

Bear hunting over bait is one western sport that allows a sportsman with physical limitations a good chance for success.

Packing out game such as a huge bull elk can quickly take the fun out of the hunt.

and a troublesome back, I no longer hunt below my camp or an access road. I'll hike uphill through the forest in the morning darkness for two hours to a promising hunting area because then I am confident that I could pack an elk out on my back since it's all downhill. But I realize that I just don't have the stamina to endure an uphill elk pack over a long distance.

The best way to avoid an excruciating pack is to pass up those hunting areas that are too far below an access road or trail. That also means setting a limit on how far from your vehicle you will hunt, to insure a pack that will not push you past your endurance. For myself, it's about three miles. For most nonresidents, it's about a mile or possibly two. Don't worry, there is a lot of good elk habitat in two forest miles, and you will probably be walking past elk at that.

Physical Limitations

Everyone has physical limitations. Even the most rugged individual has a limit that his body can by pushed to. However this section is concerned with hunters who have obvious physical limitations such as missing limbs, bad knees, or age.

There are virtually no limitations that should keep a sportsman from making his dream trip for big game in the west. Missing limbs? I know of several hunters who adapted their hunting style and area to suit their limitations and did quite well.

And then there's guys like Mike Reilly. I met Mike in Idaho while he was bowhunting bull elk — from a wheelchair! Mike was paralyzed from the waist down after a car accident, but that did not stop him from fulfilling his lifelong ambition to bowhunt bull elk with a bow and arrow.

Mike searched until he found an outfitter who could accommodate his special needs. Of primary importance was the hunting terrain. Mike needed to hunt in an area where he could wait in ambush for elk, and this outfitter has several good areas where elk trails intersected. Mike killed a big five-point bull elk after his outfitter bugled it to within five yards of Mike.

Much of the western terrain is steep and rugged, but in every state there is some prime hunting terrain suitable for a person with physical limitations. Even in my hunting grounds in Idaho and Montana, where everything looks steep and rugged, there are areas where a hunter with physical limitations could do quite well.

A hunter who is confined to a wheelchair or could not walk much would have no problem hunting antelope or mule deer in the rolling prairie country of Colorado, Wyoming, or Montana. Most of this type of hunting is done by driving slowly along dirt roads until game is spotted, and lots of shooting can be done without stalking.

Any hunter who has identified his physical limitations should make any prospective outfitter aware of them and then find out if the man can accommodate his special needs. And the guy who plans a self-guided hunt can often locate gentle terrain with good access from topographic maps. He could also mention his limitations to the wildlife biologists he calls in his search for prime hunting areas and possibly get some tips on good areas that way.

We all have physical limitations. The key here is to be aware of them and not let them ruin your hunt. And no matter what limitations you have, don't let it hold you back from making your dream hunt in the west.

Author Mike Lapinski with a whitetail buck taken on the edge of a clearcut in western Montana.

Chapter 6

CHOOSING A WESTERN HUNTING RIFLE

Nonresident hunters who have never used anything more than a 30-30 rifle or shotgun with slugs to hunt deer in the eastern wood lots must move up to a larger calibre hunting rifle for western hunting. Not only that, but they also must face the fact they will have to learn to hit game at long range with their new firearm.

Western terrain is much more open than the typical eastern woodlot, and shots up to 400 yards are considered reasonable using modern high powered rifles. Western big game also tends to be larger. Animals such as elk, moose, and bear require a calibre with quite a bit more knockdown power than a 30-30.

Fortunately, I can relate to the urban nonresident in this situation because I hunted the oak forests of Pennsylvania and the beech groves in New York for many years before I moved west. I was accustomed to dense whitetail cover and quick, short range shots at fleeing deer. The average shot at a deer was about 50 yards. A 100 yard shot was unusual — and usually missed, at least by me.

Even my preseason sighting-in procedure was typical of the close range shooting done back east. A 12 inch pie plate was set out at 50 yards, and if my bullets hit the pie plate "anywhere" the gun was good enough to kill a deer with.

The thing that impressed me immediately after my move west was the wide open spaces. Montana is nicknamed Big Sky Country, but in my opinion the entire west should have been called "big sky" country. Prairies rolled along as far as the eye could see, and mountain ranges went on and on until they faded into a haze.

That first fall when I tagged along with some local guys who'd befriended me in northern Idaho, I was shocked to see how far they'd shoot at game. Sometimes, the game was so far away that you had to first scope it to see if it had antlers! But even more shocking was the fact that these guys shot with great confidence in their 30-06's and .300 magnums and dropped big game in their tracks at (to me) astonishing distances of 300 to 400 yards. And there I stood with my 30-30 with an 18 inch barrel and open sights.

The Modern Big Game Rifle

Today's modern high powered hunting rifles can and will reach out 400 yards or more and drop the biggest bull elk in its tracks. I don't have enough fingers or toes to count the times when I watched distant elk, antelope, and deer crumple after a single shot from my hunting partner's 7mm magnum. I've even been known to make a few of those shots.

The modern big game rifle today is also constructed to withstand the tremendous chamber and action pressures associated with long range calibres. That's why the bolt action design has virtually taken over the high powered rifle market. The rigidity of action, speed of the firing pin fall, and precise breeching which supports the entire cartridge make the bolt action rifle the most accurate and reliable.

Modern Cartridge Composition

Modern cartridges reflect the special needs of western hunting conditions. Sure, there are calibres that don't even accommodate bullets as large as the 170 grain 30-30 deer load. The .270 is a good example, with a top bullet weight of 150 grains. But when you place these two cartridges side by side, the .270 dwarfs the 30-30.

The reason is the case size. The .270 casing looks grossly oversize, which is exactly what it is supposed to be. It holds a lot of powder which is needed to zip that 150 grain bullet out there in excess of 2,500 fps (feet per second). The 30-30, on the other hand, is dawdling along at about 1800 fps, and its bullet drop is astronomical at 300 yards. By comparison, the .270 bullet drop at 300 yards is about 10 inches, not enough to worry about.

Hopefully, after reading the above comparison, any urban nonresident hunter planning a western big game hunting trip will feel deservedly cowed into putting that 30-30 or .35 Remington back in the closet. He'll procure a modern big game rifle in an adequate calibre and determine to shoot it accurately.

Choosing The Right Western Calibre

There are five calibres that are favorites among western hunters. They are the .270 Winchester, 7mm Remington Magnum, 30-06 Springfield, .300 Winchester Magnum, and .338 Winchester Magnum. As I said, they

Western terrain often allows long range shots of up to 400 yards.

are the favorites, but there is also a host of other calibres that fit between, around, over, and under these favorites that are also used, depending on the game.

It is difficult to choose a perfect calibre for a western hunt because no calibre seems to have the ballistics that make it perfect for every animal. This is especially true when you consider the fact that a nonresident elk hunter in Wyoming may also be stopping along the prairie to hunt antelope on his way home. One day, he is hunting big, big game, and the next day he's trying to hit a fleet buck antelope that weighs no more than a small whitetail doe back home.

The right calibre to take on a western big game hunt will depend a lot on what type of game the hunter will be concentrating one. If he is primarily after elk, he'll be looking for a calibre who's statistics show real knockdown power even at longer ranges. If he's primarily after deer or antelope where bullet speed and drop are critical, he may opt for a lighter calibre.

With that in mind, we'll look at each of the five favorite western hunting calibres and discuss the pros and cons of each. A ballistics and trajectory chart for each calibre is also included at the end of this chapter using a 150 grain Spire point bullet fired from a 24 inch barrel. Using an identical load

The modern bolt action rifle can and will reach out 400 yards or more to knock down the biggest bull elk.

for each cartridge will quickly show differences in velocity, energy, and bullet drop between them. This type of comparison is excellent for finding out what's hot and what's not. The exception will be with the .338 magnum because bullet weights for this calibre begin at 200 grains.

The .270 Winchester

The .270 is a favorite of many western hunters because it bridges the gap between the high speed, small bullet varmint cartridges such as the .220 Swift or .243, and the bigger bore, bigger bullet cartridges such as the 30-06.

The .270 is a surprising choice of many antelope and mule deer hunters who normally do their shooting at long range. My friend Jim Monzie is a seasoned veteran of many antelope hunts on the open prairie, and Jim swears by the .270. Jim told me, "Just about any varmint rifle will kill an antelope. They're not that hard to put down when hit. The problem with varmint rifles such as the .220 Swift and even the .243 is that the small bullet loses its stability and accuracy over long range."

"Wind is a common occurrence on the prairies," Jim added. "A tiny 50 grain bullet that has to reach out 400 yards through a 20 mile per hour wind to hit an antelope might drift off target six feet before it gets there. But you take the 150 grain bullet from a .270, and there will be much less wind drift."

The 150 grain bullet is the top factory load for the .270, and this bullet weight is often found lacking among serious elk hunters. Most elk hunters like a bullet weight up around 180 grains. However, there is also a large contingent of experienced elk hunters who claim that the .270 is an excellent elk gun, and there have been too many elk killed with this calibre to state categorically that it is not adequate for elk.

The .270 is excellent for hunting antelope, deer, sheep, mountain goats, and black bears. It is an adequate calibre for elk, marginal for moose, and inadequate for grizzly bear. Generally, the ballistics of the .270 lag behind the other four favorite western calibres. The .270 has a medium recoil.

The 7mm Remington Magnum

A wise gunsmith must have heard the complaint about the .270 because the 7mm magnum was invented with a slightly larger case that could hold enough powder to push a 175 grain bullet faster than the .270 could move its 150 grain bullet.

The result was a rifle with medium recoil that could shoot flatter than the .270 for smaller game at long range, but still had the capacity to deliver a 175 grain elk load at high velocity over long range.

The 7mm Remington magnum is an excellent calibre for antelope,

The .270 Winchester is a good example of a modern long range rifle. It's bullet size is smaller than the old-fashioned 30-30, but its case is much larger. The result is more energy at long range.

deer, bighorn sheep, mountain goats, elk, moose, and black bears. It is marginal for grizzly because its top bullet weight of 175 grains is considered too light for smashing through this dangerous animal's heavy bone structure.

The 30-06 Springfield

The 30-06 is by far the most popular all around western big game hunting calibre. The hunter who uses the same rifle to hunt everything from prairie dogs to moose will find a bullet range in the 30-06 from 110 grains to 220 grains.

Another advantage of the 30-06 is that it is available in almost every type of action and in virtually every brand name. In addition, you don't have to worry about ammunition if you should happen to misplace yours during the hunt. Every gas station and small store in the boondocks stocks "odd-six" ammunition. Recoil of the 30-06 goes beyond the medium range, and leans more towards heavy.

The 30-06 Springfield is an excellent calibre for antelope (using a 150 grain bullet), deer, bighorn sheep, mountain goat, black bear, elk, and

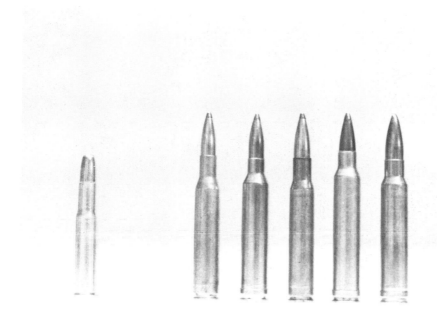

The old-fashioned 30-30 on the left is dwarfed by the five favorite western hunting cartridges. From the left, they are: .270 Winchester, 7mm Remington magnum, 30-06 Springfield, .300 Winchester magnum, .338 Winchester magnum.

moose. It is considered inadequate for grizzly because it lacks that extra punch to smash its 220 grain bullet through a grizzly's heavy bone structure.

The .300 Winchester Magnum

The .300 Winchester magnum is the big brother of the 30-06, and it is available in the same bullet weights as the 30-06. However, a slightly larger case holds enough extra powder to push .300 magnum loads faster than its little brother.

Many experienced elk hunters consider the .300 magnum to be the perfect elk gun. It has devastating knockdown power on elk even at ranges exceeding 400 yards, and the bullet drop is manageable. The recoil of a .300 magnum is considered heavy, though I don't notice much difference between the .300 magnum's kick and a 30-06.

The .300 Winchester magnum is considered an excellent calibre for antelope (150 grain bullet), deer, bighorn sheep, mountain goat, elk, and moose. It is considered adequate for grizzly bear because it has that extra punch to deal a quick killing blow with the 220 grain bullet.

The .270 Winchester is an excellent western calibre for long range shooting at thinner skinned game such as deer.

The .338 Winchester Magnum

The .338 Winchester magnum is used mostly for the heavier western big game such as elk, moose, or grizzly bear. Bullet weights begin at 200 grains and end at 300 grains. However, some hunters also use the .338 magnum on big mule deer at long range.

The specialized bullet range of the .338 magnum makes it obvious that it was not intended for lighter skinned, small bodied western game such as antelope or deer. The typical .338 magnum rifle weighs about 10 pounds, and no one climbing the crevices in bighorn sheep or mountain goat country would want to pack around all that extra weight. Recoil from the .338 magnum is considered heavy.

The .338 Winchester magnum calibre is excessive for antelope, deer, bighorn sheep, mountain goat, and black bear. It is excellent for elk, moose, and grizzly bear.

How To Sight In A Rifle

A hunter planning a western hunt should have his rifle sighted in for long range shooting. He should also do some long range target practice.

The best way to sight in your rifle is to bore sight it at 25 yards using a solid bench rest.

In addition, he should begin estimating long range distances so that he will be better able to figure out how far away various game animals are on a distant sidehill. One sure method of doing away with the guesswork of distances is to purchase a rangefinder. They are easy to use and accurate.

Bore Sighting

The first step in sighting in your new rifle is to bore sight it. Set up a solid bench rest 25 yards from the target. Set the rifle on some sandbags and then pull the bolt out of it. Look through the bore and center the target through it. Then look through the scope and move the crosshairs until they also rest on the target.

Your first shot should be from 25 yards, and you want the bullet to hit a half inch below dead center. The bullet must rise about 1.5 inches from the bore to the scope level (line of sight) to hit the target at 25 yards, and it will continue to rise to about three inches high at 100 yards.

Fine Tuning

Now for the fine tuning. Set your solid bench rest at 100 yards and see where your group is hitting. You will have to do some fine adjusting to get a perfect group, but once your rifle is consistently putting holes three inches above the bullseye at 100 yards, you can be sure that it will hit a deer at 300 yards, where bullet drop will be about eight inches.

Bullet drop

The bullet drop at long range varies with each calibre. Check the ballistics on your rifle and know how much drop it has at 400 yards. The nice thing about sighting in your rifle three inches high at 100 yards is that the bullet will not drop that much below the line of sight at 300 yards to worry about.

Long Range Shooting Tips

Many shooters miss long range shots because they hold too high over an animal's back. For instance, a hunter who shoots a 30-06 decides that at 400 yards he should hold a foot over the animal's back. It is nearly impossible to judge when the crosshairs are 12 inches above the back at that

The 30-06 Springfield is an excellent black bear calibre.

distance. Consequently, a hunter unknowingly holds five feet high and overshoots the game — even at 400 yards!

Experienced western hunters sight in their rifles to have no more bullet drop at long range (400 yards) than the chest depth of their quarry. An antelope hunter will sight in his .270 to have a 12 inch drop at 400 yards. Of course that means that the bullet will be about five inches high at 100 yards, and the hunter must hold a little low at shorter ranges. At long range, he need only place the crosshairs on the top of the back to insure a hit.

Windage

Wind drift is a problem that long range shooters should take into consideration. A bullet that travels 400 yards will be blown off course to some degree by the wind. This was never more apparent than when a client of mine took a long shot at a bull elk.

The man had great confidence in his 30-06 and informed me that he could kill any elk at 400 yards. After I watched the man target practice, I believed him. After several tough hunts, we finally found a bull feeding

The .300 Winchester magnum is considered by many experienced elk hunters to be the perfect elk gun.

Fine tune your rifle at 100 yards to see where your group is hitting.

with several cows across a drainage. From prior hunts in that area, I knew the distance to be about 375 yards. My client took two shots from a steady rest on a log — and missed both times!

We checked where the bull had been standing and found where both bullets had plowed into the ground at the correct elevation, but they were about 30 inches to the right — just enough to miss the elk. That got me looking into wind drift. I was amazed at my findings. A 180 grain bullet from a 30-06 will have a wind drift of about 40 inches at 400 yards in a 20 mph crosswind!

It's tricky making a windage allowance. However, shooting at long range often does not spook big game, and you may get several shots at the animal. If you have a steady hold, but continue to miss, take note of the wind and then compensate for it a foot at a time with each shot.

Bullet Weight And Composition

Bullet weight and composition are critical to the overall killing performance of a high powered rifle. The right gun shooting the wrong bullet often results in a less-than-perfect hunting experience. Most of the time, the rifle gets the blame when it should actually be the bullet.

A hunter once recounted an experience during which he shot a bull elk at 50 yards with a .300 magnum. The bullet hit a rib and penetrated only

Experienced western hunters sight in their rifles to have no more bullet drop at long range than the chest depth of their quarry.

far enough to destroy one lung. Fortunately, there was snow on the ground and the guy was able to track down and kill the bull a half mile away. This hunter was adamant that the .300 magnum was not a good elk gun.

The .300 magnum is an excellent elk gun. The problem was the hunter's arbitrary bullet selection. He was using a 150 grain bullet with a thin jacket. At 50 yards the bullet was screaming along at 3100 fps. When it hit the elk's rib, the thin copper jacket could not hold the lead core together, and the bullet disintegrated into tiny fragments.

The typical western big game hunting rifle will have high velocity performance, and this tends to make a bullet blow up on impact unless its composition allows for controlled expansion. It doesn't make much sense to take a gun like the .300 magnum and then shoot a light bullet at supersonic speed at a heavy bodied big game animal. A heavier bullet will deliver as much or more knockdown power, and the bullet's weight will make it more stable.

Bullet composition is critical for controlled expansion. The perfect bullet peels back into a mushroom-like blob, thereby creating more damage as the bullet moves through an animal. In the past, not enough attention was given to controlled expansion. However, bullets on the market today provide excellent controlled expansion in both handloads and factory loads.

Two bullets to keep in mind are the Nosler Partition and the Speer

Expert elk hunter Kelly Johnston always allows for wind drift when shooting long range.

Grand Slam. The Partition bullet has a solid copper partition in the middle. The front half of the bullet expands until it reaches the copper partition. The rear half of the bullet still has enough mass to keep the mushroomed half moving forward instead of fragmenting. The Partition is available in factory manufactured loads.

The handloader should consider the Grand Slam. This bullet has a copper jacket whose thickness varies from thin at the tip to heavy towards the base. The result is a thin jacket at the tip which quickly peels back upon impact, allowing proper mushroom expansion. The heavy jacket at the base of the bullet keeps the expansion under control and maintains weight at the base to keep the bullet plowing forward.

Ballistics For .300 Winchester Magnum
(150 grain Spire Point bullet fired from 24 inch barrel)

Range (yds)	Velocity (fps)	Energy (ft/lbs)
Muzzle	3,100	3,202
100	2,824	2,657
200	2,562	2,188
300	2,317	1,789
400	2,089	1,454
500	1,878	1,174

Trajectory

Range (yds)	Bullet drop from line of sight
Muzzle	− 1.5
100	+ 1.5
200	0.0
300	− 7.0
400	− 20.0
500	− 42.0

Ballistics For .270 Winchester
(150 grain Spire Point bullet fired from 24 inch barrel)

Range (yds)	Velocity (fps)	Energy (ft/lbs)
Muzzle	2,600	2,252
100	2,399	1,917
200	2,208	1,625
300	2,029	1,372
400	1,860	1,153
500	1,703	970

Trajectory
(rifle sighted in at 200 yards)

Range (yds)	Bullet location from line of sight
Muzzle	− 1.5
100	+ 2.4
200	0.0
300	− 9.5
400	− 27.6
500	− 56.2

Ballistics For .338 Winchester Magnum
(200 grain Spire Point bullet fired from 24 inch barrel)

Range (yds)	Velocity (fps)	Energy (ft/lbs)
Muzzle	3,000	3,998
100	2,759	3,381
200	2,529	2,841
300	2,312	2,375
400	2,109	1,976
500	1,919	1,636

Trajectory

Range (yds)	Bullet drop from line of sight
Muzzle	− 1.5
100	+ 1.6
200	0.0
300	− 7.2
400	− 20.9
500	− 43.1

Ballistics For 30-06 Springfield
(150 grain Spire Point bullet fired from 24 inch barrel)

Range (yds)	Velocity (fps)	Energy (ft/lbs)
Muzzle	2,900	2,802
100	2,634	2,312
200	2,384	1,894
300	2,152	1,542
400	1,935	1,248
500	1,735	1,003

Trajectory

Range (yds)	Bullet drop from line of sight
Muzzle	− 1.5
100	+ 1.8
200	0.0
300	− 8.0
400	− 24.0
500	− 49.0

Chapter 7

ARCHERY EQUIPMENT FOR A WESTERN HUNT

A nonresident bowhunter will be faced with several hunting conditions in the West unlike anything he's experienced before, and special archery equipment is necessary to adapt to the demands of the hunt. Most of the western big game is heavier than the whitetail deer back home, and the West's wide open spaces often require shots at distances that are normally passed up.

A bowhunter needs a heavier bow to hunt the heavier big game such as elk and moose. Most deer bowhunters use a bow in the 45 pound pull range, but that weight is inadequate for these larger animals. In addition, a bowhunter who is faced with longer shots must look to a heavier bow to cut down on loss of accuracy from trajectory.

Proper Western Bow Weight

Medium sized western big game such as antelope, bear, deer, sheep, goats, and lion can be hunted with the same weight bow that a nonresident used for whitetails back home. These animals are thin skinned, with only deer-like bone structures. The uncertainty begins when a nonresident plans to hunt the "bigger" western big game such as elk or moose.

The problem that many prospective elk bowhunters encounter long before their western dream hunt is that they are accustomed to hunting deer, and they experience a great deal of confusion about the correct weight bow to use on larger western game.

They realize that an elk is larger than a whitetail deer, but they wonder how much larger in terms of special equipment needs. If their favorite compound deer hunting bow set at 45 pounds zips arrows through deer back home, can they expect the same performance when they crank up the limbs 5 or 10 pounds? Or will they need a much heavier bow that

Medium sized western game such as mule deer can be bowhunted with the same weight bow that an eastern hunter uses for whitetails back home.

threatens to tear out their arm sockets at full draw?

I know the feeling. My first elk bowhunting experience occurred back in 1970 in the Clearwater River drainage of northern Idaho. I'd killed a dozen deer in Pennsylvania using a 45 pound recurve, but I'd purchased a 50 pound Shakespeare recurve in anticipation of my move to Idaho.

Fortunately, I met some local guys who were interested in bowhunting elk, and they took me along into some prime elk hunting areas. Besides the difficulty I encountered getting used to the rugged and vast Idaho forests, I was also shocked by the sheer physical makeup of a mature bull elk.

They were huge! I knew they were larger than the deer I'd hunted back east, but my first encounter with a rutting bull elk left me not only with a thrilling, nerve shattering experience, but it also left me in awe of the massive, big boned physique of an elk.

I was hunting along the banks of a stream at the base of a steep mountainside in the early morning when I heard a bugle about 400 yards above. It sounded pretty phony, and I guessed that it must have come from one of my hunting partners.

One of the guys had given me a homemade elk bugle made from black plastic pipe. It was a crude looking thing, and besides, I didn't have much faith in this notion of being able to bring in a bull elk with a flute-like whistle like you were the Pied Piper. I then did something that would change my bowhunting forever. I bugled back.

The bull came crashing down the mountainside in a furious rush, with limbs crashing and branches popping. Hooves pounded ever closer, and before I was fully prepared for it, the bull was less than 15 yards away, smashing his antlers against a large alder bush.

I crouched trembling behind a small tree, wondering if it wasn't too late to retreat. I could clearly see the bull through the alders, and I was awed by his immense physical presence. This was not a large deer, like I'd expected. This was big, big game.

The bull's large hooves actually sank into the damp forest floor. His massive shoulders and powerful neck lurched forward, and his huge antlers pounded the alders and tore them out by their roots. Another thing that impressed me were his bones. That massive shoulder blade looked as formidable as a knight's shield.

A sudden shift in the wind brought immediate silence from the bull's direction, and a moment later I was further amazed to see how quickly such a large animal could slip away into the depths of the forest.

That first elk encounter probably caused an overreaction on my part because I went right out and purchased a 70 pound recurve bow, and I killed my first three elk with it before I had to admit that it was too much bow for me. I dropped down in weight and purchased one of those newfangled compound bows made by some guy named Jennings.

Over the years, I've pondered the question of the correct bow weight to use on elk, and I must admit that I have wavered back and forth several times between light and heavy bows. Each time that I was on the verge of making a final decision on the matter, some bowhunter would relate his personal experiences that forced me to modify my opinion.

However, that nagging question still arises, and I'm asked it at least a dozen times each year. What's the best bow weight to use on elk?

I always answer that there is a difference between the "minimum" and the "best" bow weight for elk hunting. The "minimum" weight bow is the lowest that a hunter can get by with and still kill an elk. The "best" bow weight for elk is the heaviest weight that an archer can shoot comfortably and accurately.

There have been a few elk killed with bows in the 45 pound pull range, but everything must be perfect to accomplish it. The arrow must strike a stationary elk between two ribs to gain the necessary penetration. Even the movement of a walking elk is enough to impede penetration of an arrow shot from a light bow. Consequently, bows in this range are considered too light for elk.

It is tempting to suggest a minimum bow weight for hunting elk and leave it at that. However, there are a host of variables from bow design and efficiency to broadhead choice that make it difficult to come up with a

A bull in heavy timber.

single poundage figure.

The modern compound bow is a good example. Late model compounds with cam wheels and overdraw zip out arrows much faster than the same weight recurve or long bow. Consequently, a hunter with a 55 pound pull recurve bow may actually be shooting a slower bow than the guy who uses a 50 pound pull compound cam bow with overdraw.

I asked my friend and recognized bowhunting expert, Dwight Schuh, his opinion on a minimum bow weight for elk. Dwight told me, "I'm a bit uncomfortable with the idea that there should be a minimum bow weight for elk. There are too many variables such as bow design and performance, shaft selection, and broadhead design."

Dwight added, "I feel better talking about the kinetic energy necessary for proper penetration on an elk. I believe that an adequate elk hunting bow should deliver a minimum of 50 foot-pounds of energy when it strikes the chest of an elk. But even that figure carries with it a few variables, such as broadhead design and shot selection. Also, a bow that delivers minimum energy at 15 yards will have dropped off considerably at 40 yards."

Most of us bowhunters don't like to get too technical, and this talk of arrow "energy" and "foot-pounds" often leaves us confused because of the

A heavier bow weight is needed to penetrate the massive bone structure and heavy muscle of a bull elk.

physics involved. However, it takes only a little math applied to a simple equation to see if your elk archery equipment produces adequate minimum energy for elk hunting.

Energy is measured in foot-pounds, which is simply the arrow weight (mass) multiplied by the velocity of a flying arrow (feet per second). We can quickly check my hunting gear to see what its kinetic energy level is. I use a 65 pound pull Golden Eagle compound bow, which shoots a 2216 aluminum shaft at 220 ft./sec. One of my hunting arrows weighs 610 grains. (Divide the arrow weight by 223744 to convert from grains to mass. Note that weight must be converted to mass; 437 grains per ounce, 16 ounces per pound, 32 pounds per slug — a unit of mass.)

The formula for calculating the kinetic energy of a bow is:

$$KE = 1/2 \text{ MASS} \times (\text{VELOCITY})^2$$

$$KE = 1/2 \ (.0027) \times (220)^2$$

$$KE = 65.3 \text{ foot-pounds}$$

Most local bow shops now have chronographs which measure arrow speed. If you are in doubt about the archery gear that you plan to use on an elk hunting trip, have your bow speed checked and a hunting arrow weighed. Then simply plug your figures into the formula above.

The minimum compound bow weight that should be used for elk should be in the 55 pound pull range. A recurve or long bow should be around 60 pounds. I base that figure on the kinetic energy equation. A modern 55 pound pull compound bow produces the minimum 50 foot pounds of energy.

That's the minimum. The best bow weight is the heaviest that you can shoot accurately and comfortably. For me it's a 65 pound pull bow, for Dwight Schuh it's a 60 pound compound, and noted world traveler-bowhunter Chuck Adams uses an 84 pound pull compound bow.

A moose is even bigger than an elk. An adult Shiras bull moose will tip the scales at 1000 pounds, and its hide alone is a quarter of an inch thick. Consequently, an even heavier bow is necessary for this huge animal. I would suggest nothing less than a 60 pound pull compound bow, or a 65 pound pull recurve or long bow.

Heavier Bow Weights Improve Accuracy

A heavy weight bow is not necessary to kill an animal the size of an antelope, but it sure helps when you are trying to hit one. Antelope and mule deer bowhunters will be required to do shooting at ranges much longer than they are accustomed to. The heavier weight bow improves

The best bow weight for elk is the heaviest weight that an archer can shoot comfortably and accurately.

The minimum bow weight for elk should be in the 55 pound range.

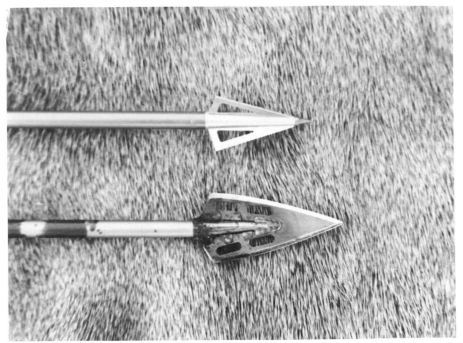

Any bowhunter who plans to use a lighter bow should pay close attention to broadhead choice.

long range shooting accuracy by cutting down on the trajectory of the arrow, and it gets it there faster, thereby exposing the flying arrow to less wind drift.

When I was first told that I'd have to take shots up to 60 yards at antelope, I was adamant. Never! My range was 30 yards and under. However, it took only a short time hunting antelope to realize that a 50 yard shot at an antelope was reasonable. In fact, most guys are lucky to get that close to these jumpy, sharp-eyed animals.

Bighorn sheep and mountain goat hunting also requires long range shooting. Chuck Adams killed a Stone sheep at 40 yards recently. Chuck said, "That was as close as I could possibly get to the ram. I shot from one bluff to another bluff where the ram was standing, and there was no traversable terrain in between. If I had my druthers, I'd shoot everything at 10 yards, but that's not always possible." Chuck added that the key to making long shots is to use a rangefinder.

The elk archer will want to beef up his bow weight into the 55 pound range or more because of the size of the animal he is hunting. The western antelope and deer bowhunter would also be smart to use a heavier bow to improve his long range accuracy. Of course, a western bowhunter should not use a bow that is too heavy for him to handle com-

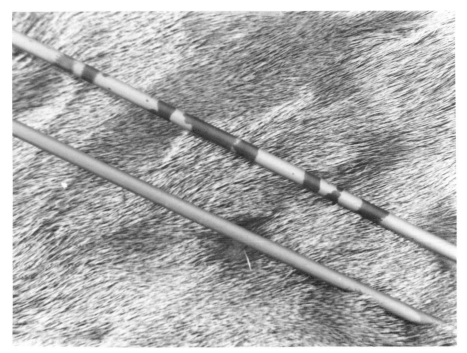

The Easton aluminum XX75 arrow shaft in burnt orange or camo are both excellent shaft choices.

fortably and accurately.

Broadhead Choice

Most broadheads on the market today are adequate for western big game hunting. However, there are noticeable differences in penetration among broadheads, and any bowhunter who is planning to use a lighter bow should pay close attention to his choice of broadheads.

Anyone who plans to use a minimum bow weight for elk or moose would be wise to consider using a flat, needle-pointed broadhead such as the Zwickey, Bear, or Magnus type heads. These broadheads generally produce greater penetration than the more common bullet shaped broadheads because they cut at the instant of impact and do not force the hide apart before the cutting blades are encountered.

That's not to say that the bullet-shaped broadheads are inefficient. These types of heads have excellent flight stability and have created a more responsible society of bowhunters because of their factory razor-sharpened blades. I use Rocky Mountain Razor three-blade broadheads, and I've killed a dozen elk with these heads. But then, I also shoot a heavier bow.

A more sturdy arrow shaft such as the Easton aluminum XX75 is perfect for bowhunting in rugged western terrain.

Hunting Arrows

You can kill the biggest bull moose in the west with one of those inexpensive aluminum arrows sold in discount stores. The shaft is nothing more than the deliverer of the deadly broadhead. However, this is over simplifying the purpose of one of the important tools of the bowhunter that an archer often overlooks.

Shaft Selection

Like I said most inexpensive aluminum arrows are straight enough to insure reasonably accurate flight. The problem is that they bend easily, and then you're fighting through walls of brush and often slipping and falling in the rugged mountains, an inexpensive shaft such as a Gamegetter aluminum arrow can take on a permanent bend.

They also might get stepped on. A couple years back, I had three men from Minnesota out to Montana to bowhunt for elk. Two of the men were using the top grade XX75 aluminum arrows, while one of the men was using the softer aluminum Gamegetter arrows. While the men were stumbling out of the tent in the dark one morning, the Gamegetter arrows got stepped on, along with one of the bows that had XX75 shafts in its bow quiver. The Gamegetter arrows had a definite kink in them, but the XX75 shafts were still perfect.

I've taken several nasty falls while pursuing elk through the rugged Bitterroot Mountains along the Montana/Idaho border, and twice my entire body weight came down on the arrows in my quiver. Not once were any bent, and that's the best reason for using the higher quality arrow shafts for your western big game hunt.

Shaft Colors

A camouflage pattern is the latest coloration craze for hunting arrows, and many bowhunters are attracted to this idea. After all, they think, if I dress up in camo to blend in with the forest, why not do the same thing with my arrow shafts? Sounds like a reasonable deduction, but there are some problems with this type of thinking.

A bowhunter should blend in well with his surroundings, but the half dozen arrow shafts in a bow quiver do not have a great impact on a bowhunter's visibilty to game animals. There simply isn't enough surface area to be detected.

Of course, a hunter wants to avoid an obvious stark color difference from his surroundings, such as white shafts. But they don't have to be invisible, either. In fact, an arrow that is too well camouflaged can create more problems than it will solve.

After a shot, it is critical that a bowhunter find his arrow and inspect it

Burnt orange is an excellent shaft color to use in snow because it contrasts well against the white background.

for blood. He might not be able to tell if he hit the animal under low light conditions until he inspects the shaft. In addition, he will be able to tell accurately what kind of a hit was made by the type of blood and matter on the shaft. Bright red frothy blood indicates a lung hit, while dark red blood indicates a hit farther back, etc.

Many wise bowhunters choose a burnt orange coloration on their hunting shafts for this reason. The burnt orange arrows blend in well with the forest (animals don't see colors well), but the bowhunter will be able to find the orange shaft even in heavy brush. I've used burnt orange aluminum arrows for many years, and I've been able to locate one of these shafts even when only an inch or two of the shaft was visible above ground.

Whitetail deer have expanded their range in much of the West and have become a popular secondary target in the region.

Chapter 8

CLOTHING FOR A WESTERN HUNT

The Rocky Mountain West in fall can be a serenely beautiful wilderness paradise when the sun is shining. In one short hour that tranquility can quickly turn into unbearable blustery winds, driving rain or sleet, or even snow as early as August. The hunter who is lulled into carelessness by this deceptively tranquil landscape of the west in good weather will pay dearly in terms of discomfort. It might ruin his hunt, or the consequences can even turn tragic.

The West experiences definite seasonal weather patterns. The summer season is known for its beautiful sunny weather, with only a few rain showers to keep the land fresh. This summer seasonal weather pattern often runs into September when most archery seasons begin, and bowhunters especially are prone to experience one of the stark realities of the Rocky Mountains in fall — unpredictable weather.

Three years ago the West experienced typical late summer balmy weather, and as Montana's archery season approached that first week in September, most bowhunters were hoping for a storm system to cool things off and make the woods more quiet. They got their wish, and more!

The first morning of archery season dawned gloomy, with a light drizzle. Every archer was pleased. An hour later, the drizzle had turned into a drenching torrent with 30 mile per hour winds, and most sane bowhunters were driven out of the woods. For the next 22 days it rained, and the forest was awash with water soaked brush and slippery ground. Any bowhunter who did not have the proper clothing simply couldn't stand the bone chilling cascade of water every minute of the day.

Of course, an alternative to fighting inclement weather is to stay indoors until good weather. That's what most of my bowhunting friends did three

Weather in the Rocky Mountain West in fall can be serenely beautiful one hour, and blizzard conditions the next hour.

The rifle hunter who is prepared for bad weather can expect better hunting overall.

years ago. They told me that there was no rush, that the elk would still be bugling when the rain stopped. They were wrong. The elk had been in full rut during the stormy weather, and by the time the sun appeared and dried the forest out, the rut was just about over.

I hunted during that stormy period because I had the proper clothing, and I killed a nice five-point bull. It seems like I'm always wet when I kill a bull elk with bow and arrow. But then, that makes sense because that's when hunting is best.

Bull elk often rut only in early morning and late evening during warm weather. When the sun appears an hour after dawn, the bulls seek shelter in heavy cover and quit bugling. But when a stormy day cames along, it seems to trigger an added vigor to their rutting instincts, and I've heard elk bugle all day during a dismal, rainy day when I was the only bowhunter outdoors.

Rifle hunters who are prepared for inclement weather can also expect better hunting overall. The hunter who is dressed to stay in the field when a storm moves in will discover a flurry of activity among big game animals as they try to fill their bellies before the storm.

Snowstorms especially are prime times to be hunting. The animals are not as wary, and whenever there is a small break in the storm, the game

A light Gortex lined boot is excellent for early season hunting.

will be feeding in the open. I took a Minnesota client on an elk hunt two years ago during a snow storm, and we almost stepped on several elk seeking shelter in a spruce thicket. A half hour later, the snow stopped, and the openings were full of feeding elk. The man shot a 5X5 bull. While we were field dressing the elk, several hunters who'd waited out the storm came by to admire the trophy. One of those men said it best, "I guess we should have been out hunting instead of drinking coffee."

Archery Clothing

Typical September weather in the West is brisk and frosty in the morning, but warm in the afternoon. Temperatures can climb as high as 80 degrees in the early afternoon, even in the high country. By late afternoon, however, temperatures will have dropped into the 50 degree range. This creates an obvious problem for the bowhunter — freeze in the morning and roast in the afternoon.

Bowhunters who will be sitting in a blind most of the day waiting for antelope don't have too much problem. They can wear heavy clothing during the brisk morning hours and then shed it when the temperature rises. Most clear weather blind hunters wear cotton camouflage clothing, with a heavy wool camo sweater worn in the morning.

The bowhunter who must hike a long distance over rough terrain during the day has more of a problem. He does not have the luxury of being able to shed bulky outer clothing because he has no comfortable way to carry it. Most bowhunters after elk or mule deer stick to light camo clothing, but they also wear a down or polypropylene vest to ward off the chill of first light. These vests can be rolled up into a small bundle and stored in a fanny pack later in the day when the temperature rises.

Footwear

A light boot is excellent for early season bowhunting. Even in hot weather, a light boot is advisable to wearing running shoes. The rugged western terrain is hard on tender feet, and the added support of a boot will help a bowhunter avoid sprained ankles and badly bruised feet. Even when hunting the prairie country for antelope or mule deer, boots are advisable. There are all sorts of sharp spined plants and cactii that go right through a canvas shoe, but a boot will ward them off.

I would advise any bowhunter to consider a light pair of boots with Gortex liners. This liner will breath away body heat, but keep feet dry if a sudden storm should hit or the ground cover is wet with morning dew.

Raingear

Raingear is a must for the bowhunter. Early fall storm systems can drench an entire archery season, and the archer who is not prepared to hunt comfortably in wet weather might just as well throw away his game tags.

Adequate raingear is one item that nonresident bowhunters always seem to be lacking in. It got so bad that I finally purchased three sets of top quality raingear to loan to clients. I'd tell them to bring raingear, and they'd show up with a cheap vinyl poncho that cost $6.95! In the cold rain, the brush tore that kind of rain gear to shreds in an hour.

By adequate raingear, I mean a complete waterproof outfit of boots, pants, jacket, and hat. A bowhunter can hunt hard all day in wet weather dressed in those items and not feel any discomfort due to the inclement weather.

The very best raingear is Gortex. It not only sheds water, but it also allows body perspiration to escape an overheated body. I consider it a miracle fabric, and I believe that it has radically changed the potential for hunting in bad weather. You can outfit yourself from head to toe in Gortex raingear. That, in fact, is what I do. I wear Gortex boots, Gortex pants, Gortex jacket, and Gortex Jones-style hat. Dressed like that I feel as carefree as a duck in the water.

Beside Gortex raingear, there are also several other major brands of raingear that is adequate. Most of these have nylon fabric with vinyl coating. They are adequate, but they do not allow body heat to escape. After a period of exertion, clothing will be damp from perspiration, but the hunter will at least be warm.

Early Season Rifle Hunting

Medium wool clothing is best for early season big game hunting. Morning temperatures in October may range as low as the teens in the western Rockies, but afternoon temperatures will climb back up above freezing.

Clothing made from wool is better than any of the new miracle synthetic fibers. Sure, some of these fibers might retain body heat a little better than wool when dry, but they sure don't do it when they are wet.

Fall hunting is prone to the whims of unstable weather patterns sweeping in from the West Coast, and cold rain or wet snow are not unusual. Consequently, you stand a good chance of getting wet unexpectedly. And if you're a long way from camp, the danger of hypothermia is real unless your clothing will retain your body heat when wet.

I've done a lot of experimenting with synthetic fibers in hunting clothing. Clothing made from these fabrics hold in heat well, and I would recommend such clothing if you are doing a lot of standing or waiting in a blind in cold, dry weather.

The problem with synthetic fabric is that they hold in body heat too well. Any exertion and a hunter feels uncomfortably warm. But when they get wet, they actually wick away crucial body heat. Wool, on the

Adequate raingear is necessary because an entire hunting trip may take place during rainy weather.

An insulated rubber boot with an Air-bob sole is excellent for hiking through deep snow over steep, frozen ground.

other hand, will keep a hunter warm even when it is soaked.

Avoid clothing with goose down unless you are planning to be stationary for a long time in cold, clear weather. Goose down clothing is too warm, when climbing through rough terrain, and it is useless and dangerous when wet.

Footwear

A pair of lightweight insulated boots with Gortex liner is advisable for early fall hunting. No matter what weather you hunt in, this type of boot will keep your feet warm and dry. Extreme cold weather is unusual in October even in the west, but if a freak cold front should move through, it would be best to bring along a pair of sturdy insulated rubber pacs.

Clothing For Late Season Hunting

Cold weather and snow are common in November in the West. Most experienced hunters use heavy wool clothing to stay warm and ward off snow. Wool long johns, pants and shirt, plus a heavy double-weight wool coat will protect a hunter from just about any weather conditions in the West.

Heavy wool clothing can't be beat for cold weather hunting in snow.

A wool cap with long bill to keep snow out of the hunter's face should also be used instead of a stocking cap. In addition, a pair of insulated five fingered gloves with Gortex liner are advisable to keep hands warm, yet functional, even in the worst weather. This is one area where wool should be avoided. Wool gloves in snow pick up too much moisture and become uncomfortable. It is also difficult to keep fingers warm when wool gloves become wet in cold weather.

Footwear

Insulated rubber boots are best for deep snow, cold weather hunting. The grip on the sole is of vital importance to a hunter who will be hiking in snow through steep terrain. A light ripple or chain link design does not have enough grip to keep a hunter's feet from constantly sliding out from underneath him.

Most of my outfitting took place in steep mountainous terrain, and I quickly discovered that clients from states where most of the hunting was on flat ground had great difficulty staying on their feet. Most of this problem was due to the very light grip on their boot soles.

I began recommending to my clients that they purchase a rubber insulated boot with a unique gripping sole called the Air-Bob. Tiny, bullet-like projections stick out from the sole and heel of the boot to individually grip frozen ground or snow. This is an invention directed towards the western hunter, and the Air-Bob sole is found on boots mostly in western sporting goods stores.

Chapter 9

PLANNING FOR OUTDOOR EMERGENCIES

Two men went hunting last November along the foothills of the Selway-Bitterroot Wilderness Area on the Montana side. The men were nonresidents stationed at an air base in Montana, and they took leave for a week of elk hunting. The men brought along all the correct provisions for anything the western mountains had to throw at them. They had a complete camping outfit, good sleeping bags, and plenty of food.

The men went hunting in an area that got hit with blizzard conditions and heavy snowfall while they were there. When the men did not return home, authorities were alerted and a search was begun. Searchers quickly located their vehicle parked at the end of an access road to the wilderness.

That was six months ago, and now that the snow is melting in late spring, searchers will again go into the mountains to try to locate some clue as to what happened to the men. One thing, however, was clear from the beginning of the search. Though the men had plenty of survival gear, they had left it all in their vehicle when they departed for their ill-fated hunt.

Anyone planning a western big game hunting trip should be aware of the potential for emergency situations. A wool shirt on your back and a candy bar in your pocket simply is not enough to insure your safe return if everything does not go according to plan.

The West is big country, and distances between roads are much farther than the nonresident is accustomed to. So when unforeseen problems arise, a hunter can't always take a quick hike out of the mountains to safety. When you take the West's large size and add to it the unpredictable western weather patterns, you have the daily potential for an emergency situation because a hunter will almost always be a mile or more from safety.

There are a host of factors that have led up to tragic situations in the

Anyone planning a western hunt should be aware of the potential for emergencies.

Rocky Mountains in recent years, but none have been more responsible than the weather. Western days in fall can turn from balmy to raging blizzards in a matter of hours. Even a rainstorm can mean trouble for the unprepared hunter because a radical drop in temperature always follows fall storms in the West.

Such unexpected situations that the nonresident hunter may be confronted with in the West do not necessarily become emergencies. Surely, a simple thing like a rain shower in itself is not cause for alarm, but add the fact that the hunter gets lost in his haste to get out of the weather, and you have an inconvenience bordering on a problem. The borderline problem becomes an emergency when the hunter has not thought out how he could survive in the rain if he had to spend the night in the mountains.

Hypothermia

Blaming the weather for the disturbing number of tragedies that occur every fall in the western states is probably misleading. Weather doesn't kill men. Neither does hunger or thirst. The West is not so big that men go on and on until they starve to death. The major cause of death among outdoorsmen is hypothermia, and it is more deadly than the meanest grizzly bear.

At least with a grizzly, you can identify your problem and try to deal with it. Hypothermia, on the other hand, slowly seeps into an unsuspecting man's body and saps him of his life-giving heat before he is aware of its danger.

Hypothermia is nothing more than the lowering of the body's temperature from the normal of 98.6 degrees. Mix cold, wet, and windy conditions with the unwary person, and the result could develop into hypothermia and death. To understand hypothermia, the effects of cold on the body must be recognized. The body's first response to cold is constriction of the surface blood vessels in the skin, soon spreading to the tissue beneath. The restricted flow of blood in these tissues slows the heat transported from the core of the body. This, in turn, results in the lowering of skin temperature and then decreasing the temperature of the body's extremities. Shivering starts shortly after the initial constriction of surface blood vessels. If heat loss continues, temperature of the body's inner core begins to drop and the following symptoms occur:

99-96 degrees — Shivering becomes intense and uncontrollable. The ability to perform complex tasks diminishes.

95-91 degrees — Violent shivering persists. Speech becomes vague, slow and slurred. Amnesia may appear.

90-86 degrees — Shivering decreases followed by muscular rigidity. Erratic or jerky movements signal poor muscular coordination. The victim may have total amnesia, but he will maintain a general appearance and posture of psychological contact.

85-81 degrees — The victim becomes irrational, loses contact with his environment and falls into a stupor.

80-78 degrees — Victim becomes unconscious and most reflexes cease to function. Heartbeat become erratic.

Below 78 degrees — Cardiac and respiratory control centers of the brain fail, followed by death.

Death by hypothermia doesn't have to be the result of a howling blizzard either. Sometimes it occurs under such seemingly innocent circimstances that the death of a human being seems ridiculous. Take the incident with John, a young, strong hiker who went on a hiking trip with several friends in the high country in July.

The weather forecast for that weekend was not ideal. A slight weather system was supposed to be moving through that region later in the day, but that news did not dampen the spirits of the hikers as they began their trek under blue skies and sunshine. Later in the day, bad weather drifted in. First, a foggy overcast covered the blue sky. Then the wind came up, and a gentle mist began. The temperature dropped to about 50 degrees.

Not everyone in the party was as physically fit as John, so frequent rest stops were called. John became chilled while resting, so he always wanted to keep charging on. His companions urged him to put on some

The bowhunter dressed in light cotton clothing may experience hypothermia when a sudden storm soaks him.

extra clothes and stay with the group, but he didn't want to drag them out and disturb his backpack. So he left the others and plunged ahead. "Sure it's getting chilly," he told them, "but it's only about 50 degrees or so. Nothing serious."

As the day progressed, the weather worsened. But nobody thought much of it, especially John. About 2 p.m. John began to shiver. But he'd shivered before, so he didn't think much of it. About then, his companions noticed his slower and more forced movements. They were actually gaining on him. They talked to him, but he either murmured something unintelligible or didn't respond at all. They thought he was mad at them. They all agreed, "If he wants to be such a he-man, let him suffer."

Suddenly John slowed to a stop in the middle of the trail. "What's wrong?" they asked. No answer. They sat him down, thinking he needed a rest. Something was seriously wrong with John, but nobody knew what. They wrapped him in a coat, but it was too late. John lost consciousness and died an hour later, in the middle of the summer at 50 degrees.

Identify Potential Emergencies

Always assess a western hunt for the potential for emergency situations.

The lure of the trophy bull elk often leads hunters into remote backcountry where emergency conditions become acute.

Most outdoor tragedies could have been avoided if those victims had just spent a few minutes quietly thinking out the potential hazards of their upcoming outings and then took a few precautions.

Look for the obvious areas of concern and identify them. For instance, will camp be a long distance from the hunting area? Will the hunt be in high altitude, rugged terrain? Will the hunt be on flat, brushy ground where it may be easy to get turned around?

Taking Emergency Precautions

Once you have identified the potential problem areas during your upcoming hunt, plan to take precautions to deal with that particular emergency. Obviously, these precautions will come in the form of an emergency kit which will contain equipment to deal with unfavorable situations.

Bowhunters especially balk at the idea of carrying along a bulky pack which might encumber their flexibility and shooting style. I carry a large fanny pack which contains everything I need for field dressing game, plus it contains an emergency kit. It sits back behind me, and I don't even think about it being there while I'm hunting. Rifle hunters can also carry a fanny pack, but most use a small daybag.

Emergency Kit

My emergency kit contains everything that I think will help sustain my life if I'm unable to get to safety. The kit contains:
1-space blanket
1-pound high energy food
1-rollup rain poncho
1-small can juice
1-pack waterproof matches
1-small flashlight
1-map of area
1-compass
1-6X8 foot sheet of orange plastic

The total weight of this emergency kit is three pounds. With it, I believe that I can survive anything the West has to throw at me. I should mention the reason for the 6X8 foot sheet of orange plastic. This dimension makes an excellent pup tent that a man can crawl under when stranded in bad weather. Also, the orange color makes your position easy to locate from the air if you are unable to move.

Dealing With An Emergency

The way that a sportsman deals with a problem in the field is vital to insure that hysteria doesn't create a tragedy out of something that was a

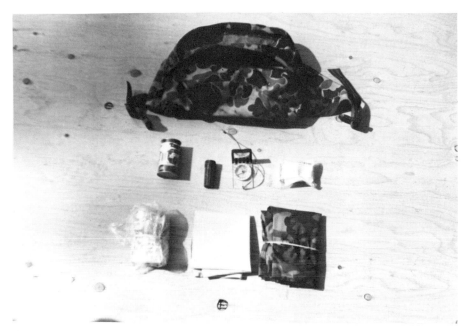

An emergency kit will occupy a small part of a hunter's pack, but it may save a hunter's life.

mere inconvenience. Take the situation that three snowshoers found themselves in a few years back in northern Idaho.

The men went snowshoeing after a fresh snow in an area of dense forest and steep mountains, but it was a well roaded area with quite a few residences nearby. In all, the men were never more than a mile and a half from a traveled road.

The big mistake the men made was to bring along brandy to bolster their spirits. The alcohol affected their reasoning so that when they got turned around, they panicked and began snowshoeing furiously forward, with no thought as to which way was out. The men became soaked in sweat and then exhausted, hypothermia set in, and they died — one of them just 400 yards from a farmhouse. There were other obvious errors that the men made, such as wearing denim clothes in the snow, but the fact remains that if the men had stayed calm and reasoned out their situation, they could have simply backtracked on their snowshoe trail to safety.

Panic

Panic is the root of all evil in the outdoors. Sure, hypothermia is the condition that results in death to the human body, but panic is usually the reason why hypothermia occurred in the first place. Men like to be in control of their lives, and when they find themselves in a situation in the

A small plastic tarp can provide a quick emergency lean-to to escape the elements.

woods, such as being lost, they want out, now!

Normally intelligent men have been found, ridiculously close to safety, dead from exposure. Searchers often find where the dead man had charged round and round in a large circle in his panicked rush to escape his predicament. One such incident occurred in which the man had died within easy hearing distance of a major four lane freeway!

I can also relate one incident where two men found themselves in a dire situation and lived to tell about it because they kept their heads and took desperate actions to match their alarming situation.

The men had gone hunting in the rugged central Idaho backcountry on horseback, and were surprised on an exposed ridge a long way from their vehicle when a sudden, vicious blizzard hit the high country. The men had not brought along emergency provisions, and the fury of the snowstorm made it quickly apparent that they could not survive for long in the elements.

The men were quickly becoming numb in the bitter cold and high wind as they discussed their rapidly deteriorating chances for surviving the ordeal. They kept their heads and took the only action that would insure their survival. Each man put a gun to his horse's head and pulled the trigger.

The men quickly gutted their beloved horses and crawled numbly inside the steaming hot body cavity, where they stayed putridly warm.

Definitely, it was a sad thing to kill the horse, but the   men were cool enough to realize that that was the only way they would survive, and they did.

If you determine that you have a problem while in the field, take five minutes to sit down and reason out your problem. If you are lost, think about how you got there. Think about possible landmarks that you might have overlooked. Determine the best action to take, whether it is best to keep on moving or stay put and set up an emergency camp. This latter course of action has saved more lives of lost men than anything else.

For every lost hunter who dies in the western wilds every year, there are dozens who have been saved because they didn't panic and charge forward into the night where exhaustion and hypothermia surely awaited them. Instead, they started a small fire and huddled around it until morning. Oftentimes, these men were able to get their bearings at first light and hike out on their own.

Hiking To Safety When Lost

There are two methods of hiking to safety that usually will take a man out of the wilderness even when he does not know where he is. The man who has no compass and no idea which way to go to reach safety should follow a large ridge or stream and stay with it until he walks out to safety.

Even though the West is big country, it's not so big that a man can't hike out of any wilderness area in two day's hiking. Take the Selway Bitterroot Wilderness Area in central Idaho. It's the largest wilderness area in the lower states, yet it is only 20 miles across at its widest point. Any man in reasonable condition should be able to hike out of the Selway Wilderness in two days, if he doesn't start going in circles.

That's why a ridge or stream is the best travel route for a lost hiker. Sure, they might meander a bit from a straight line, but generally, they will proceed on an orderly course, and it's only a matter of time before civilization is encountered.

A large ridge is best for traveling because the hiking is easier. In addition, a hiker will also be able to see better and he might be able to locate a hunting camp or road from above. The next choice would be a large stream. Avoid the urge to drop off a ridge into a small creek bottom. Small creeks are usually choked with blowdown, and a hiker will be slowed considerably and quickly exhausted.

Compass Use

A compass is an invaluable tool for the sportsman who doesn't want to get lost. However, a compass is of no use if a hunter doesn't have a map to go along with it. It's of no use to look at a compass and determine

A compass is an invaluable tool for the sportsman who doesn't want to get lost.

magnetic north if you don't have a map which shows the way you have to go to get back to safety.

If you don't have a map when you are about to leave a vehicle to go hunting in a rugged area, at least take a compass reading on the road you just traveled. That way if you get turned around, you will at least know which direction to travel to get back to the road and safety.

I've been all over the West in the backcountry, and have to admit that I still get lost. I also still find myself in miserable weather conditions that I had not expected. And once in a while there are physical problems, like when I lost my eyeglasses five miles from camp (I'm almost blind as a bat without them!)

Sure, I worry when I get into an unpleasant or irritating situation, but I've learned not to panic because my emergency kit is always with me in the backcountry. I feel that I have everything in it to keep me alive, and any nonresident hunter should not leave camp without an emergency kit of their own. The darn things are lifesavers!

The mountain goat might be limited in its availability but it still attracts its share of die-hard hunters. The goat makes a dramatically beautiful trophy.

Chapter 10

WESTERN EQUIPMENT NEEDS

The equipment that a nonresident hunter must bring out west with him depends a lot on the type of hunting that he is doing. Obviously, the fully guided hunter will not be required to bring out pots and pans and tents and food. That's what he pays an outfitter for. On the other hand, a group of hunters who hire an outfitter for a drop camp hunt may have to bring along a few more items, such as field dressing accessories, food, or bathing and sleeping facilities. Of course, hunters who plan an unguided hunt are totally responsible to bring every single item of camping gear, food, and hunting accessories necessary for a decent western hunt.

Transportation

The one concern that all nonresident hunters have is transportation. It doesn't matter whether you book a fully guided hunt or plan a self-guided hunt, you still need some form of transportation out west. However, every hunter has certain alternatives in transportation that may prove best for him.

Airlines

The hunter who is planning a fully guided hunt would be wise to consider making the trip out west by plane, especially if he lives a long distance away and is strapped for time. A hunter from Florida who books a guided hunt in Idaho has got a three-day trip facing him each way. Anything can go wrong along the way, and valuable hunting time could be lost while a disabled vehicle is slowly repaired in some small town in the middle of nowhere.

On the other hand, air transportation is a matter of hours from Florida

The guided hunter needs only a rifle to achieve a successful hunt with this bull elk, but the unguided hunter is totally responsible for all camping gear, food, and hunting accessories.

to Idaho (Yes, there are airports even in Idaho!). I'm not so sure that air transportation isn't at least as economical as vehicle transportation when you consider the cost of gas, meals, and lodging along the way, plus the wear and tear on the vehicle.

When I outfitted, half my clients came by plane, and I was surprised how smoothly things went. Airlines were able to easily accommodate clients with deer, bear, and elk to take back home. I just had to tape empty shotgun shells over the tips of antlers to avoid damage to other freight. The meat was always cut and packaged at a local butcher shop and then frozen. That way, there was no chance of meat spoilage during the flight, and the frozen meat was easy to package in cardboard boxes. The entire load of antlers, hides, and frozen meat was shipped back home on the same flight with the client as air freight at a nominal cost.

Trucks

Nonresident hunters who plan a drop camp hunt with an outfitter might not be able to take a plane flight out west if there are too many accessories to bring along. And if they have to bring in their own food, they will almost certainly need to bring it out with them by pickup truck. However, if food and sleeping bags are furnished, drop camp hunters might still be able to come by plane.

The nonresident hunter who plans a self-guided hunt will be responsible for transporting a lot of gear, and he will need a sturdy pickup that will not only provide transportation out and back, but also handle the rough use (sometime abuse) common to western backcountry roads.

I hope all you antelope hunters are not flipping through these pages as if vehicle choice doesn't concern you. The mistaken impression that many antelope hunters have is that most of the hunting is done on gravel roads, and just about any pickup truck will do. That's true if the weather stays dry, but the gumbo clay of the western prairie country that is hard as a rock in dry weather is almost impossible to drive through with a two-wheel drive pickup when it is wet.

I was hunting antelope in eastern Montana last year, and I met four New York residents who were using a two-wheel drive pickup. The men proudly showed me two antelope that they had bagged during the first two days of their hunt. The night of that second day, it started raining, and the next day I had to be careful where I drove my big four wheel drive pickup to keep from getting stuck.

The men in the two-wheel drive truck promptly got stuck and had to pay a wrecker $100 to get them to a paved road. They were floundered for the remaining four days of their hunt and were forced to kill doe antelope and mule deer to fill their tags because those were the only animals that stayed close to the paved roads.

Any nonresident hunters who will be using their own vehicles for hunting transportation should bring out a four-wheel drive pickup. Backcoun-

A tent is an inexpensive camping shelter, and some hunters say that it's the best way to experience the excitement of western hunting.

try roads are notorious for losing their bottoms when the weather turns wet. And if it isn't rain, it's snow!

Camping Gear

Unguided hunters need enough camping gear to furnish a reasonably comfortable camp. Basically this gear should furnish adequate shelter, food, and warmth. Careful planning can avoid a lot of misery during the hunt.

Trailers

A self-contained, pull-along trailer or motorhome are excellent shelters if you already have one. Of course, not many men can got out and purchase one of these expensive RV's just for a seven day hunt. One of the nicest things about trailers is that everything is already in place and you don't have to spend hours fighting tent pegs and ropes. Also, camp can be quickly moved when a better hunting spot is located.

Tents

A tent is an inexpensive camping shelter, and some sportsmen feel that it is also the best way to appreciate the western experience. They say that exciting hunting tales around a blazing campfire every night in front of a tent takes a hunter back to the basics of what the western hunting experience is all about.

Another big advantage of tent camping is that it can be packed in and set up far from roads and away from congested hunting areas. It sounds like a lot of work, but a three man party packing in a camp a mile from a road can pack everything in two round trips in about two hours.

The best way to tent camp is with two tents. One tent is used for sleeping, and the other tent is used for cooking and drying clothes. The wet weather that so often accompanies hunting season leaves hunters with the problem of drying clothes, and with one tent, this simple process can be disastrous. Wet weather will also douse any ideas about cooking out under the stars, and that second cooking tent will be greatly appreciated during stormy weather.

Hunters who intend to pack in their camp to a good hunting area would be wise to use a lighter umbrella-type tent. These tents only weigh about 30 pounds. Hunters with horses can afford to pack in the heavier canvas wall tents. These are the preferred tents of outfitters because of their sturdiness and complete waterproof construction.

Food

I have three friends from the Midwest who come out to Idaho every year to bowhunt for elk. Their wives get together and create a complete menu for the men during their stay, and the ladies precook everything. This food is then frozen and brought out in coolers.

These men use a tent camper and usually park at the end of an old logging road. Consequently, they don't have to worry about the weight of their food because they won't be packing anything more than a small lunch in the field. In fact, for the camper in a trailer or motorhome, anything goes in the line of food, though the way my friends handled this chore seems to be the best way to eat inexpensively.

Hunters who intend to pack in a camp must be more concerned with both the weight and perishable potential of their food. Freeze dried foods are very light and the new line of camping foods are delicious. Water is essential when cooking freeze dried foods, so make sure there is a water source nearby. Plan to pack in a collapsible five gallon water jug for camp water and cooking.

Campstoves And Heaters

A two burner Coleman gas stove is ideal for cooking, but it should not be used to dry clothes or as a heating stove. The Coleman cook stove wasn't designed to be a heater and won't produce enough heat anyway.

A five-pound sleeping bag is an excellent all-around choice for the western hunter. It will roll up into a small pack, yet keep the hunter warm in below zero temperatures.

An unattended open flame is also a sure way to create a disaster in camp.

Most hunters who use umbrella tents use a kerosene heater for warmth and for drying wet clothes. Kerosene is virtually odorless, and its protected flame makes it a safe choice for a heater. Hunters with wall tents sometimes use a kerosene heater, but usually they use a sheet metal wood stove. These are excellent for both cooking and heat, but dry firewood is often a problem if the woods are wet.

Sleeping Bags

A five pound sleeping bag will keep a man comfortably warm down to about -5 degrees Fahrenheit. Early season hunters should not be concerned about such a heavy bag being too warm for September camping. No matter how warm it is during the day, western nights are always cool.

Bathing Facilities

Hunters need to bathe regularly no matter what the weather. In the heat of early season, perspiration needs to be washed off to keep human scent to a minimum. In cold weather, a hunter gets to itching constantly if he does not bathe daily.

Bathing can be done in any kind of weather by sponge bathing. The usual procedure is to heat a large basin of water, and then use a sponge to wash down the hair and body. It sounds like a crude way to bath, but let me assure you, after a hard day of hunting, there is nothing like a hot sponge bath to revitalize a tired body.

Basic Camping List

A good basic camping list for three men would include:
2 tents (wall or umbrella) 10X10
3 sleeping bags
1 Coleman cook stove (at least two-burner)
1 kerosene heater
3 sets eating utensils
1 set cooking utensils
2 gas lanterns
1 tarp (cover game, etc.)
1 large basin for sponge bath
1 large basin for dishes
1 5 gallon water jug
1 shovel for fire, latrine

Field Dressing Equipment

Drop camp and self-guided hunters must carry with them enough field

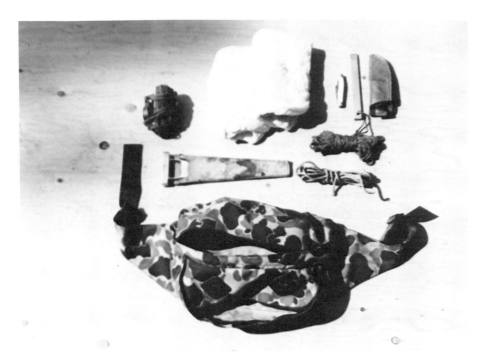

My field dressing kit contains four nylon game bags, game saw, rope, two knives, sharpening steel, plus pulley — and it only weighs three pounds.

dressing tools to get the job done. This may not be a big problem for an antelope hunter who shoots his trophy close to a road, but for the back-country elk hunter, it is a big chore. A downed elk is very difficult to field dress, quarter, and then hang to cool the meat. A hunter needs a complete selection of field dressing utensils to cut down on unnecessary work.

I carry a big fanny pack with a large pocket on top, and another one on the bottom. My emergency kit goes in the top pocket, and my field dressing kit goes in the bottom one. The total weight of the pack is six pounds and it contains everything that I would need to survive an emergency or field dress and hang meat in the middle of nowhere. My field dressing kit contains:

4 large nylon game bags
2 heavy duty knives
1 game saw
1 sharpening steel
30 ft. light rope
1 small pulley for hoisting bagged meat

Binoculars

Alan Brockway is an experienced western big game hunter, and he had

The small binoculars on the right are an excellent choice for the western hunter. They fit into a shirt pocket and are always available for quick use.

this comment about binoculars. "Next to my rifle, I choose my binoculars as my most important hunting accessory. I only started using binoculars three years ago, and I wonder now how much game I passed up before that because I was either too tired or too lazy to look at it through my rifle scope. I know that I'm a better hunter now that I use binoculars."

Binoculars are a vital necessity for the western big game hunter. Every far away shadow or suspicious movement should be glassed with binoculars. It's amazing how often a hunter carrying a scoped rifle slung over his shoulder will pass up these suspicious objects because he gets tired of taking his rifle off his shoulder.

Bowhunters also have a critical need for a good pair of binoculars. I carry a small pair of binoculars when I go bowhunting, and I glass not only far away objects, but I also glass suspicious movements or tan colors only 50 yards away. Many times a quick look through my binoculars has alerted me to game up ahead before I stumbled forward and spooked it.

Binoculars come in all makes and sizes, but a good pair of binoculars should be practical and functional to be of any use to a hunter. That means they should not be so powerful that all images are a shaky blur, and they should be small enough to be easy to carry and use.

Most experienced hunters carry seven power compact binoculars. They are easy to see through and small enough to stay out of the way when not in use. Alan Brockway told me that he uses a pair of Zeiss folding compact binoculars. My personal choice is a pair of Bushnell Custom Compact binoculars in 7X26 size. These small binoculars fit snugly inside my breast pocket, and I can quickly pull them out, glass a suspicious object, and replace them with one simple hand movement. Avoid inexpensive binoculars. Their optics are poor, and I've found that you usually can't get both lenses focused to your eyes at the same time.

Appendix A

Appendix A is a state-by-state reference to the best proven game producing areas for each big game species. Use this appendix to begin your search for a specific hunting spot. First contact should be to that state's regional wildlife agency.

ARIZONA

Antelope

With a few exceptions, Arizona's antelope herds generally inhabit the open flats and cedar/juniper country throughout the north and central parts of the state.

1.) In the northwestern part of the state, there is good antelope hunting beginning about 20 miles west of Page on U.S. 89A at the north end of the Navajo Indian Reservation. This area runs through the Kaibab and Uinkaret Plateaus for about 130 miles and ends north of Grand Canyon National Park.

2.) In the northcentral part of the state, a surefire spot is north of Seligman on U.S. 66. This area about 120 miles west of Flagstaff is known for its trophy sized bucks.

3.) In the central part of the state, good antelope hunting is found north of Prescott in Yavapai County on both sides of U.S. 89 for 40 miles. This area is about 100 miles southwest of Flagstaff.

4.) Another good antelope area is east of Prescott between U.S. 89 and I-17. This area is about 115 miles south of Flagstaff.

5.) Good antelope hunting is found west of Prescott between U.S. 89 and the Santa Maria River in the Chino and Big Chino Valleys.

6.) One of the best areas is in the westcentral part of the state around Alpine on both sides of U.S. 666 in Greenlee County. Springerville to the north has been especially productive over the years, as has the St. Johns, Holbrook, and Winslow Areas.

Black Bear

1.) The forested mountains in the Flagstaff area are prime bear habitat, especially east and south.

2.) The Apache Indian Reservation west of Phoenix is another area of mountainous, forested terrain where black bears in huntable numbers are found.

3.) The Mogollan Rim country north of the Fort Apache Indian Reservation is a good area to find black bears, especially in the Tonta Basin and Verde River drainages.

Deer

Arizona has three types of deer to hunt: Rocky Mountain mule deer, desert mule deer, and Coues whitetail deer. Most hunters concentrate on the Rocky Mountain mule deer because it averages 50 pounds more in weight. It is also taller and darker than its desert cousin. Rocky Mountain mule deer range is in the northern half of the state from the Arizona Strip country south to the Mogollan Rim, where the desert mule deer takes over, and it inhabits the central and southern lowlands. Coues deer are located in the extreme southeast.

1.) The best Rocky Mountain mule deer area is in the remote Arizona strip country, with some 3.5 million acres of public land north of the Grand Canyon. Because this area is so far from the major population centers of Phoenix and Tucson, hunting pressure is light and the bucks grow big. Specifically, look to the foothills of Black Rock, Mud Mountain, Parashant Plateau, Pakoon, and Mount Logan.

2.) Next door to the Arizona Strip is the Kaibab Plateau north of the Grand Canyon. This is excellent muley country. This sprawling, pine-clad plateau is laced with roads to facilitate access. Specifically, hunt around Wild Horse Park and Dead Horse Mesa near Jacob Lake on U.S. 89A.

3.) Another good Kaibab area is near Jolly Sink and along Big Ridge close to the upper end of Orderville Canyon.

4.) A good desert mule deer area lies south of Flagstaff and west of Show Low. Units 6A and 6B, east and north of Camp Verde are particularly promising. The rugged desert/mountain country on both sides of I-17 near Black Mesa and Black Canyon look good.

5.) A good area for Coues deer and desert muleys is in the foothills of the Galiure, Graham, and Chiricahua Mountains (units 31 and 32) in Cochise county in the southeast corner of the state.

Elk

1.) One of the best elk areas in the state is located north and east of Springerville on U.S. 666 in South Apache County and further south to Alpine.

2.) Another good elk area takes in the mountains just north of the Fort Apache Indian Reservation. This also includes the reservation, which allows limited hunting on a fee basis.

3.) In the northern part of the state, elk in good numbers are found just north of the Grand Canyon on the Kaibob Plateau south of Jacob Lake on U.S. 89A.

4.) The Mogollan Rim country which extends north of the Fort Apache Indian Reservation is always good for elk. Best hunting is south of U.S. 66 below Holbrod in Sitgreaves National Forest.

5.) The high forests immediately east and south of Flagstaff on I-17 in Coconino County are excellent for elk.

Mountain Lion

The best lion hunting counties are Gila, Coconino, Cochise, and Yavapai. The area south of Tucson also produces steadily, especially below Atacosa Mountain in the Coronado National Forest. A nonresident lion hunter should hire a guide with lion hounds. Lions are rarely seen without the use of dogs.

Bighorn Sheep

Arizona has the much coveted desert bighorn sheep. In recent years, about 70 permits have been issued, with 10% going to nonresidents. Success is about 50%. The best areas are in the extreme west and southwest, from Kingman on U.S. 66 in south Mohave

County to the Kofa Mountains north of Yuma. A few permits are also issued for areas southwest of Phoenix and the mountains surrounding Tucson.

Rocky Mountain Goat

Arizona has no viable goat population.

Moose

Arizona has no viable moose population.

COLORADO

Antelope

1.) The northwest units 3 and 4 primarily in Moffat County provide the best habitat and biggest trophy antelope. This is mostly public land.

2.) There is excellent antelope hunting in the northeast and northern plains units A-12 and A-13 just south of the Wyoming border which includes the Pawnee National Grasslands.

3.) Big trophy antelope are found in the Chico Basin east of Colorado Springs in El Paso and Lincoln Counties.

4.) Good antelope hunting is found northeast of Fort Collins on U.S. 287 in Weld County in the northern part of the state.

5.) Another good area for antelope hunting is located in eastern Lincoln County near the towns of Hugo and Limon on U.S. 40.

Black Bear

Bait and hound hunters account for most of the bears taken in Colorado (75%). Hunters on their own usually kill bears while hunting for other game such as elk.

1.) One of the best bear areas is in northern Colorado from Steamboat Springs in Routt and Jackson Counties north to the Wyoming border, especially along the Continental Divide.

2.) Good bear hunting in western Colorado can be found west of Montrose on U.S. 50 in the Uncompahgre Plateau area.

3.) Another good bear area can be found north of Pagosa Springs on U.S. 160 in Archuleta County in the San Juan Mountains along the Continental Divide in Hinsdale and Mineral Counties.

4.) In the southwest corner of the state there is good bear hunting just west of Silverton on U.S. 50 in Dolores and San Miguel Counties.

5.) In southcentral Colorado, you can find bears along the Continental Divide east of Saguache on U.S. 285 in Saguache County.

6.) In the south, excellent bear hunting is found southeast of Salida on U.S. 50 in Fremont County in the Sangre De Cristo Mountains.

Mule Deer

The southwest corner of Colorado in the San Juan National Forest has more trophy size mule deer than any other area of similar size, and a quick look at the record will prove it. The top 10 hunting units in Colorado which have consistently produced three-point or bigger mule deer are:

1.) Unit-62 on the east side of the Uncompahgre Plateau in the southwest corner of the state, west of Delta on U. S. 50 (42% success rate).

2.) Unit-22 in the Piceance Creek Basin in the northwestern part of the state. Hunter success is 48%, and often 100 deer per day may be seen.

3.) Unit-61 on the west side of Uncompahgre Plateau northeast of Unraven. Hunter success is 39%. This is Kirt Darner's favorite hunting area.

4.) Unit-20 in the Estes Park area of the Front Range Mountains 60 miles west of Denver. Hunter success is 45%.

5.) Unit-70 in San Migual County south of Naturita in the southwest corner of the state. Hunter success is 39%.

6.) Unit-11 in the Strawberry Creek drainage, southwest of Craig in Moffat County in the northwestern corner of the state. Hunter success is 49%.

7.) Unit-40 at Glade Park in Mesa County, southwest of Grand Junction in the western part of the state. Hunter success is 42%.

This unit is considered the best in the state for trophy bucks.

8.) Unit-21 in the Douglas Creek drainage in Rio Blanco County in the northwestern part of the state. Hunter success is 54%.

9.) Unit-71 in Dolores County, north of Cortez in the Dolores River drainage of the San Juan National Forest in the southwestern part of the state. Hunter success is 27%.

10.) Unit-35 in the Castle Rock area north of Eagle in Eagle County in the White River National Forest in the northcentral part of the state. Hunter success is 47%.

Whitetail

The eastern prairie along the Kansas border is best for whitetails in all the river bottoms (mixed with muleys). Specifically, try the Arkansas River from Boonecast to Cold on the Kansas line; Purgatory River from Las Alamas south; Republic River from Genoa east.

Elk

The northwestern and southwestern areas of Colorado produce its tremendous elk herds. Herds in the north are more localized, with large elkless areas in between them. In the southwest, terrain is more suitable, so the elk are more evenly distributed. The top 10 elk hunting counties are Rio Blanco (unit 12), Routt (unit 14), Gunnison (unit 23), La Plata (unit 24), Archuleta (unit 74), Larimer (unit 76), Mineral, Eagle, Grand, and Hinsdale.

1.) In the southwestern part of the state, one of the best elk hunting areas is around the Purgatory Ski Area in unit 74 in the San Juan Mountains. This area is located 25 miles north of Durango on U.S. 550 in La Plata County. Take F.S. road 578 from U.S. 550, which leads to Purgatory.

2.) In the southwest, another good area is found due north of Pagosa Springs on U.S. 160 in Archuleta County all the way to the Continental Divide. Also, the area north and south of Vallecito Reservoir is good for elk.

3.) A vast herd of elk inhabit the Flat Tops Wilderness Area on the White River Plateau in the White River National Forest. Try Piceance and Yellow creeks south of the White River and southwest of Meeker on U.S. 13-789 in Rio Blanco County.

4.) The entire area around Steamboat Springs on U.S. 40 in Routt County is excellent for elk. This area is located in the Routt National Forest. Specifically, try Elk Creek north of Steamboat Springs, and Trout Creek to the south.

5.) In the southwest, good elk hunting is found in the Uncompahgre Plateau area of the Uncompahgre National Forest. Try the area southwest of Delta and Montrose on U.S. 50 in Montrose County. This is high, wild country.

Mountain Lion

The best counties in Colorado for hunting mountain lion are Rio Blanco and Los

Animas. A nonresident lion hunter should hire a guide with dogs. Lions are rarely seen without the aid of dogs.

Bighorn Sheep

Colorado has a sheep population of about 500, and hunters harvest about 50 each fall. Back in the 1950's the sheep population had risen to 5,000, but disease drastically reduced the herd. Sheep are on the upswing again, and it is reasonable to expect many more sheep hunting opportunities in the future. The best sheep hunting areas are in the Poudre River drainage and Pikes Peak. Sheep Creek and Cimarron creeks are also good, as is the Blanco River and Battlemont area.

Rocky Mountain Goat

Goats are not native to Colorado, but a transplant herd has blossomed to about 500 animals, and about 40 permits are issued annually. The best area for goats is on Mount Evans north of Granton on U.S. 285. Success in this area has hit 100% in the past. The Collegiate Mountain Range is also good and boasts a 70% success rate. Also, the Eagles Nest Wilderness Area is good for goat hunting along the Gore Mountains Range near Avon.

Moose

Colorado is not prime moose country. A few wander down from Wyoming occassionally, but there is not enough population to allow hunting.

IDAHO

Antelope

Idaho's antelope herds are loacted in the southeastern part of the state. The best counties are Lemhi, Jefferson, Bingham, Lincoln, and Blain. Unlike other western states, Idaho's antelope herds are found on vast tracts of public land where private land limitations do not exist.

1.) Lemhi County west of Salmon is especially interesting for antelope hunting. This northernmost antelope county has lots of broken land, and antelope can be hunted much like deer. Stalks and close range shooting often result.

2.) One of the best antelope counties is Custer County east of U.S. 93A on both sides of the Pahsimeroi River.

3.) Another excellent antelope county is Clark County west of Dubois on I-15 in Birch Creek Valley.

4.) Good antelope hunting can be found in Bingham County north of the Fort Hall Indian Reservation.

5.) The chances of bagging a trophy antelope are high north and east of Shoshone on U.S. 93 in Lincoln County.

Black Bear

The entire mountainous terrain north of Sun Valley in southcentral Idaho is excellent bear range clear to the Canadian border. That's why Idaho's bear harvest is the largest in the West. Bait and hounds are legal, but hunters on their own also fare well.

1.) An excellent bear hunting area is located in Hell's Canyon National Recreation Area north of Weiser on U.S. 95 in Washington County along the Oregon Border.

2.) Excellent bear hunting can be found in the Lochsa River drainage east of Kooskia on U.S. 12 in Clearwater County in eastcentral Idaho. Bear hunting doesn't get much better than this area, and it's a favorite for hound hunters.

3.) Prime bear habitat can be found in the Elk City area in Idaho County and north into the Selway-Bitterroot Wilderness Area. Lots of berries and lots of bears in this area.

4.) A top bear producer in northcentral Idaho is the entire Clearwater River drainage east of Orofino on U.S. 95A in Clearwater County. Specifically, try the mountains north of Elk River, and around Pierce and west to the Montana border.

5.) Excellent bear hunting is found in the entire St. Joe River drainage in the St. Joe National Forest east of St. Maries on U.S. 95A in Benewah County. The upper St. Joe country east of Avery is especially productive for bears all the way to the Montana border. Another good side drainage is the North Fork St. Joe River north of Avery.

6.) There are lots of bears in the Coeur d'Alene River drainage north of Kingston on I-90 in Shoshone County in northern Idaho. This is heavily timbered, brushy terrain, and bears are everywhere. Especially try the hills around the McGee Ranger Station on the North Fork of the Coeur d'Alene River. This is on the Coeur d'Alene National Forest.

Mule Deer

The biggest mule deer are found in southern Idaho from Burley in Cassia County east to the Wyoming border. However, mule deer are also found in north Idaho in the higher mountain elevations, with whitetails in the bottoms.

1.) In the southeastern part of the state, particularly that area east of I-15 at Pocatello is a roughly rectangular area 60 miles by 180 miles. This area occupies only about 14% of the total Idaho land mass, yet it has yielded over 40% of the state's Boone and Crockett mule deer bucks. This strip of land is aptly named the "Super Buck Strip." Just three counties have provided eight of the most recent record book entries — Bear Lake, Franklin, and Bonneville.

2.) Another good area for big muley bucks is in the Hell's Canyon National Recreation Area north of Weiser on U.S. 95 in Washington County along the Oregon border. This area takes in the rugged Snake River drainage.

3.) Excellent trophy mule deer hunting can be found west of McCall in Adams County and north Washington County. Several Boone and Crockett bucks have come out of this area.

4.) There are lots of heavy beamed trophy muley bucks in the far reaches of the Salmon Mountain Range in northern Lemhi County (units 21 and 21A) in eastcentral Idaho.

5.) One especially productive mule deer area is in unit 67 immediately north of Swan Valley. This area averages a whopping five buck kills per square mile. Also, south Lemhi County east of the Pashimeroi River boats three buck kills per square mile.

Whitetail Deer

Whitetail deer are heavily and evenly distributed north of the Salmon River country. Virtually every hillside and creek bottom has a good population of whitetails, but Benewah and Kootenai counties in northern Idaho have a reputation for producing lots of nice four point bucks.

Elk

It doesn't do justice to this state to name a few drainages and leave the reader with the impression that those are the only good spots for elk. Virtually all of the forested land north of Sun Valley is good elk country. The exception is the area north of Pend Oreille Lake near the Canadian border, which has a light elk population. Some following descriptions may seem vague, but the intent is to show the widespread heavy distribution of elk in those areas. Statistically, the top three elk producing areas are Chamberlain Basin, the Lochsa River, and the Selway River, all in northcentral Idaho.

1.) In the eastcentral part of the state, the vast Selway-Bitterroot Wilderness Area is the top elk producer. The Lochsa, Selway, and Clearwater River drainages are evenly matched for productivity throughout. Two good jumping off points are the towns of Kooskia on state route 13, and Elk City on state route 14. This is rugged backcountry with very limited road access.

2.) In the central part of the state, the River Of No Return Wilderness is one of the top elk hunting areas. This area lies due south of the Selway-Bitterroot Wilderness. Best areas are the Hell's Half Acre area, along with the area around Deep Creek campground. Excellent hunting can also be found down the Selway River drainage and to the north around Beaver Jack and Cayuse Mountains.

3.) In the western part of the state, the Hell's Canyon Recreation Area along the Oregon border is excellent for elk. This area takes in the Snake River drainage north of Weiser on U.S. 95 in Washington County.

4.) The entire North Fork Clearwater drainage north of the town of Pierce on state route 10 in Clearwater County is very good elk hunting. Elk are virtually everywhere, and good hunting can be found near roads. Try Kelly Creek north of the Kelly Creek Ranger Station, and Black Canyon for good elk hunting. This area is in the Clearwater National Forest.

5.) Excellent elk hunting can be found in northern Idaho in the entire St. Joe River drainage east of St. Maries on U.S. 95A in Benewah County. In particular, try the upper St. Joe country east of Avery all the way to its headwaters at St. Joe Lake. Every side drainage of the St. Joe has good elk herds.

6.) Another excellent area for elk hunting in north Idaho lies in the entire Coeur D'Alene River drainage north of Kingston on I-90 in Kootenai County. In particular try the area around the McGee Ranger Station and north. This area lies in the Coeur D'Alene National Forest.

Mountain Lion

The best lion hunting areas are in the Clearwater and Salmon River drainages in northcentral Idaho. In northern Idaho, the St. Joe River drainage also has a good population of big cats. A nonresident lion hunter should hire a guide with lion hounds. Lions are rarely seen without the aid of hounds.

Bighorn Sheep

The greatest numbers of bighorn sheep are found in the Salmon River drainage, especially along the Middle Fork. The best spots are the Camas Creek-Loon Creek region of the Middle Fork, the Big Creek Area farther north and west of the Middle Fork. There are some backcountry sheep units in the Salmon River drainage that allow unlimited hunting. However, these are very remote units, some of which have seen no sheep taken in a season from hundreds of permit holders.

Rocky Mountain Goats

Goats are plentiful in the high regions of the Salmon River in central Idaho. Other healthy goat herds are located in the Clearwater and St. Joe River drainages in north Idaho.

Moose

About 230 moose are killed annually, for a hunter success of 89%. The best moose county is Fremont west of Yellowstone National Park. The upper Clearwater country between the Lochsa and Selway River drainages is also excellent moose country. Other good moose areas lie in the North Fork Clearwater, the Salmon, and the St. Joe River drainages.

MONTANA

Antelope

The entire eastern half of the state east of the Continental Divide is prime antelope habitat, and multiple permits are often a necessity in some areas to control the huge antelope herds. The southwestern area of the state near Dillon also has good antelope hunting.

1.) In the southeastern part of the state, Beaverhead and Madison counties on both sides of U.S. 91 south to the Idaho/Wyoming borders have good antelope hunting. Concentrate on the rolling prairie around the towns of Dillon and Twin Bridges.

2.) In the northcentral part of the state, there are lots of antelope in Fergus and Petroleum counties north and east of Lewistown to Grassrange and south along Flat Willow Creek.

3.) In the southcentral part of the state, excellent trophy antelope hunting can be found in Golden Valley County west of Roundup to Harlowton. Also in that area, good hunting can be found in Stillwater County north of Laurel, and Musselshell County east of Roundup.

4.) In the northeastern corner of the state, there is good antelope hunting found in Phillips County east of Fort Belknap Indian Reservation and south of Malta along U.S. 191. Another good spot is found in Valley County east of Fort Peck Indian Reservation and north of Glasgow along Montana route 24. McCone County to the east of the reservation is also good.

5.) In the southeastern corner of the state is found the heaviest concentrations of antelope. In fact, over 14,000 either-sex licenses are issued for the area east of Billings to the North Dakota border, and sometimes a hunter can kill up to four extra antelope. The area around Miles City is especially productive.

Black Bear

The entire western half of Montana from Livingston all the way to the Idaho border is bear country, and the closer you get to the border, the better the bear hunting gets. Also, several central mountain ranges such as the Bear Paw, Big Snowy, and Little Belt mountains all harbor healthy bear populations. The very best Montana bear hunting is found in the dense forests along the Idaho line. Bear baiting and hound hunting are not allowed in Montana, but hunters on their own do very well by glassing open slopes for bears.

1.) In central Montana, there is good bear hunting found south of Lewistown in Fergus County in the Big Snowy Mountains.

2.) In southcentral Montana, there is good bear hunting in the rugged Absaroka Mountain Range which runs south from Livingston on I-90 in Park County to Yellowstone National Park. Concentrate of the eastern side of U.S. 89 for the best bear hunting, and use caution because grizzlies frequent this area.

3.) In southern Montana, there is very good bear hunting found in the Gallatin River Canyon which runs for 60 miles south from Belgrade on U.S. 191 to Yellowstone National Park. Be sure to make a positive bear identification because grizzlies also frequent this canyon.

4.) In southwestern Montana, the West Fork Bitterroot River south of Darby on U.S. 93 in Ravalli County is excellent bear hunting. Also, the West Fork Bitterroot River northwest of nearby Sula is good bear hunting.

5.) In the western part of the state, the entire area north and south of interstate 90 from the Idaho border east to Alberton in Mineral County is excellent bear hunting.

6.) In the northwestern corner of the state, both sides of U.S. 2 from the Idaho line to Libby and Kalispell are excellent for bear. Also, the Yaak River north of nearby Troy is good for bears, as is state route 37 north of Libby all the way to Eureka. This area offers the best bear hunting in the state.

Mule Deer

Mule deer live throughout Montana, from the eastern prairie to the rugged western mountains. In the west, muleys are found at mid level and up in the mountains, and whitetails are located in the bottoms. In the eastern part of the state, muleys like the open sagebrush country, while the whitetails like the secluded thickets in the river bottoms.

1.) In the central part of the state, one of the best mule deer areas is in the Musselshell River drainage in Golden Valley, Wheatland, and Musselshell counties until it empties into Fort Peck Reservoir. Virtually anywhere along this drainage is top muley country, and extra deer tags are often available for this area.

2.) In the northcentral part of the state, a top mule deer area is found in the Missouri River drainage from Helena through the counties of Meagher, Judith Basin, and Fergus to the Fort Peck reservoir. This is commonly called "the mule deer belt" and multiple deer tags are often issued.

3.) A good area for mule deer in the western part of the state is in the Cabinet Mountains Wilderness Area south of Libby on U.S. 2 in Lincoln County. There are lots of big heavy-beamed muleys found at timberline in these mountains.

4.) In southwestern Montana, one area that is really tops is in the Madison and Jefferson River drainages in Madison, Silver Bow, and Jefferson counties. Deer populations are very high.

5.) In the southeastern part of the state, the Custer National Forest south of Miles City on I-90 in Custer County has excellent mule deer hunting and usually some multiple tags.

Whitetail Deer

Montana has more whitetails in the record book than any other western state. Low to nonexistent hunting pressure allows these deer the chance to grow to trophy size. Look especially in Missoula, Lincoln, and Lake counties in western Montana for trophy sized whitetail bucks.

Elk

Montana has so many excellent elk hunting areas that you could hunt almost anywhere southwest of Bozeman and west of Butte and not go wrong. Generally, the western forests hold the largest populations of elk, but there are a few isolated mountain ranges in the central part of the state such as the Big Snowy, and Bear Paw mountains that are also excellent elk hunting. Some of the following descriptions may seem a bit generalized, but in certain areas vast tracts of forest are prime elk habitat and elk hunting is excellent throughout.

1.) In the far western part of the state, the entire Bitterroot Mountain Range along the Idaho line from the Canadian border south to Yellowstone National Park is all excellent elk hunting. I should know, that's my stomping grounds. One really good spot lies west and south of Thompson Falls on U.S. 200 in Sanders County. Another top spot is the Great Burn Wilderness Area south of Superior and Alberton in Mineral County.

2.) In western Montana, the most productive and famous elk hunting area is the Bob Marshall Wilderness southeast of Kalispell on U.S. 93 in Flathead County. The area around and south of Spotted Bear Ranger Station on the Flathead National Forest is a good place to center your search for a good elk hunting spot, but the Bob Marshall is good elk hunting throughout.

3.) In the southwest area, the mountains south and west of Darby on U.S. 93 in Ravalli County which comprise the Montana half of the Selway-Bitterrot Wilderness Area is an excellent elk hunting spot.

4.) In central Montana, the Big Belt and Little Belt mountains east of Helena on U.S. 91 in Lewis & Clark County provide big bulls every year. The Augusta area near Wolf Creek is also good.

5.) In southcentral Montana, the Gallatin River drainage south of Belgrade on U.S. 191 in Gallatin County is excellent for trophy bulls, as is the Yellowstone River drainage to the east. These twin drainages receive a large flow of migrating Yellowstone elk each November, and many big bulls are killed.

6.) In the southwestern part of the state, the Madison and Jefferson River drainages north and south of Ennis on U.S. 287 in Madison County are top elk producers.

7.) In the southwest, the Anaconda-Pintler Wilderness north of Wisdom in the Big Hole River drainage is excellent for trophy bull elk.

Mountain Lion

The northwestern corner of Montana offers the best mountain lion hunting. The areas around Libby, Kalispell, Trout Creek, Thompson Falls, and Superior are all excellent for lion hunting. A nonresident lion hunter should hire a guide with lion hounds. Lions are rarely seen without the aid of dogs.

Bighorn Sheep

About 600 bighorns are harvested in Montana annually, and any nonresident planning a Montana hunt should apply for one of these coveted sheep permits. Sheep permits are offered on a drawing basis through much of the state, but the highest sheep kill comes from the unlimited sheep hunting area north of Yellowstone National Park in the Absaroka Mountains. In addition, many sheep permits are issued for the far west area north of Plains and Thompson Falls on U.S. 200 in Sanders County.

Rocky Mountain Goats

About 600 goats are killed annually, mostly in the unlimited sheep hunting area north of Yellowstone National Park. However, a smattering of goat permits are issued throughout the western half of the state. Any nonresident planning a Montana big game hunt should apply for one of these goat permits in an area closest to where he will be hunting.

Moose

The best moose hunting is in the general area west of Yellowstone National Park. Also good hunting for moose can be found in the Centennial Valley near Red Rocks Lakes Wildlife Refuge in southwestern Montana. In the northwest, the country around Thompson Falls and Libby is good for moose. Montana offers many moose permits, and the nonresident hunter should apply for one in the area he intends to hunt.

Grizzly Bear

Grizzly bear hunting in Montana is limited to the northwestern part of the state in the Bob Marshall ecosystem. A healthy and growing grizzly population exists in this area, and there is a possibility that even more grizzly hunting will be allowed in the near future. In addition, Montana now has a new policy of allowing hunters to harvest problem bears in other areas of the state. The hunter who is picked to deal with one of these problem bears almost always takes home a trophy.

NEVADA

Antelope

There is only limited antelope hunting allowed in Nevada, most of which occurs in the northwest corner of the state.

Black Bear

There is no viable bear population in Nevada.

Mule Deer

The surprising statistic about mule deer hunting in Nevada is that 40% of all bucks harvested were 4 points or better. The top deer producing counties are Elko, White Pine, Nye, Washoe, and Humboldt.

1.) The Humboldt National Forest produces lots of big bucks every year in its northeast regions.

2.) The Jarbridge Wilderness Area north of Elko is especially good for big bucks.

3.) In the central part of the state, the Toiyobe National Forest has excellent muley hunting between Austin and Tonopah.

4.) Paradise Valley in Humboldt County and Smith Valley in Lyon County are two good deer hunting areas that need the deer herd trimmed every year to avoid crop damage.

Elk

There is only a small elk herd in Nevada, with only a handful of permits issued to residents.

Mountain Lion

The best lion hunting areas are around Jarbridge and Wassuk, and in the Stillwater Mountains. A lion hunter should hire a guide with hounds. Lions are rarely seen without the aid of dogs.

Bighorn Sheep

There is no viable sheep herd in Nevada.

Rocky Mountain Goat

There is no viable goat herd in Nevada.

Moose

There is no viable moose population in Nevada.

NEW MEXICO

Antelope

The northeastern region of the state has the best hunting in both quantity and quality. The bucks there are also bigger compared with other areas of the state. The southeast part of the state also provides good antelope hunting.

1.) In the northeastern area, the country around Springer produces an abundance of trophy antelope bucks, especially south along U.S. 84-85 to Wagon Mound.

2.) The string of towns Clayton, Capulin, and Raton on U.S. 64-87 are excellent for antelope hunting all the way east to the Texas/Colorado line, and west to Springer and Wagon Mound.

3.)In eastern New Mexico good antelope hunting can be found near Tucumcari near the Texas border, and farther south on U.S. 54.

4.) In the western part of the state, the area around Magdalena on U.S. 60 and southwest to the Gila National Forest is also prime antelope country. This is about as far west as an antelope hunter would want to go because the far western part of the state becomes mountainous and is given over to elk.

5.) In southeastern New Mexico, excellent hunting can be found from Carlsbad on U.S. 285 west and south to the Texas border. Look specifically for good hunting in the Staked Plains area.

Black Bear

The best black bear hunting is found in the northern and southwest corners of the state in the high mountains of the Continental Divide.

1.) In the southwest, one of the best bear hunting areas is located in the greener areas north of I-10 to the north of Separ in Grant County.

2.) In the northern part of the state, the Jicarilla Indian Reservation and surrounding mountains has a huntable bear population.

3.) In the north, the Sangre De Cristo Mountains west of Vermejo Park in Colfax County from the Colorado line south to Eagle Nest has a decent bear population.

4.) Good bear country can be found in the Castilla region, specifically the mountains between Santa Fe and Taos.

5.) In the southcentral part of the state, there is good bear hunting found in the San Juan and Jemez mountains west of Los Alamos. Also, the Sacramento Mountains in the Lincoln National Forest near Cloudcroft and the Gila drainage north of Silver City is good for bears.

Mule Deer

The best trophy mule deer hunting is found in the Santa Fe and Carson National Forests. The heaviest concentrations of muleys are in the arid southeastern and southwestern mountains.

1.) In the north near the Colorado border, there are lots of big mule deer in the Oso Canyon (unit 2) north of U.S. 64 and east of the Jicarilla Indian Reservation.

2.) In the southwest, the rugged desert-like foothills of the Black Range, between Quemada and Hillsboro, gives up many big bucks annually. Hunt south of U.S. 60 and west of I-25.

3.) In the central part of the state, the scrubby lowlands of the Datil and Gallinas mountains north of Magdalena in Socorro County has good deer hunting. Hunt north of U.S. 60.

4.) In the southwest, lots of nice bucks are found in the Cabello Mountains southeast of Truth Or Consequences in Sierra County east of U.S. 85.

5.) In northwestern New Mexico, the Cruces Basin area is one of the best spots in the state for muley bucks. The best access to Cruces Basin is F.S. road 87, west off U.S. 85 in Arriba County.

Coues Deer

This diminutive whitetail is located in the southwest corner of the state below Lordsburg in Hilldale County south of I-10. Also, look around Animas or Deming in Luna County south of I-10.

Elk

The best elk hunting is found in northern New Mexico in the high rugged mountains of the Continental Divide. Several huge private ranches and Indian Reservations allow controlled hunting for elk and are fast gaining a reputation for providing record book trophy hunting.

1.) In the north, one of the best public hunting areas is in the northern and central part of Rio Arriba County south of Chama on U.S. 84. Another good spot in this area extends from Chama due east into Taos County to just west of the Rio Grande River.

2.) In the north, six state-owned Fish & Wildlife Areas (units 4 and 55) are tops for elk. They are the Humphries, Sargent, Uracca, Valle Vidal, and the Colin Neblet north and south. The Valley Vidal area has been averaging a 5-point or better bull elk harvest in recent years.

3.) Some of the best hunting in the state is in the Carson and Santa Fe National Forests. Top spots are the area surrounding Chama on U.S. 84 in Rio Arriba County; Tres Piedras on the western edge of the Carson N.F. Another good spot is around the village of Tres Piedras on U.S. 85 west of Taos County.

4.) In the northern part of the state, the Carson National Forest near Questa and the Red River drainage east of Tres Piedras on state route 38 is good for big bulls. The Pecos area in the south end of the Santa Fe National Forest, east of the city of Santa Fe, is also good for elk. In addition, Taos and the Eagles Nest area to the north produce some nice bulls.

5.) The Jicarilla Indian Reservation, headquartered out of Dulce, offers exclusive fee trophy bull elk hunting.

6.) Another private trophy hunting enterprise is the vast Moreno Ranch in Northern New Mexico. This 50,000 acre ranch boasts a harvest record of 68% bulls which went 5X5 or better. Also, the Vermejo Park Cattle Ranch offers exclusive trophy elk hunts.

Mountain Lion

The best lion hunting is in the Guadalupe Mountains and the Gila National Forest. A nonresident lion hunter should hire a guide with lion hounds. Lions are rarely seen without the use of hounds.

Bighorn Sheep

Both Rocky Mountain and desert bighorn sheep exist in small numbers in New Mexico. Only a token amount of permits are issued annually, mostly in the Sandia Mountains.

Rocky Mountain Goat

New Mexico has no viable goat herd.

Moose

There is no viable moose population in New Mexico.

OREGON

Antelope

The antelope herd in Oregon is not large, and limited permits are available. Most of the antelope are found in the southeastern portions of Deschutes, Crooks, and Grant counties, and the southern part of Klamath, plus much of Lake, Harney, and Malheur counties. Presently, only residents are allowed to hunt antelope.

Black Bear

The best bear producing areas are in the far western coastal rain forests. Other traditionally good bear areas include the extreme southwestern and extreme northeastern corners of the state.

1.) In the far western part of the state along the coast, the Newport/Waldport/Florence areas furnish the highest bear kills. Try both sides of U.S. 101 between these towns.

2.) In the extreme southwest, the area east of Port Orford and Gold Beach is an excellent bear hunting area. Bear populations are very dense.

3.) In the extreme northeastern corner of the state, there is good bear hunting from LaGrande in Baker County north along the Blue Mountains to the Washington border.

4.) In the eastern part of the state, good bear hunting is found north of Austin in Grant County along the rugged Blue Mountains.

5.) In the far east, the Hell's Canyon National Recreation Area along the Idaho line has excellent bear hunting. This rugged area is accessible by taking Oregon route 82 east out of Enterprise, where the Forest Service has a recreation headquarters.

6.) Prime bear habitat is found in the Cascade Mountain Range which runs north from Crater Lake National Park. The mountains near the Washington border at Mount Hood are especially good bear hunting.

Mule Deer

Central Oregon offers the best chance for a trophy mule deer buck, especially Crook, Deschutes, Lake, and Grant counties.

1.) In the eastern part of the state, the Hell's Canyon National Recreation Area along the Idaho border harbors lots of big mule deer. This rugged area is accessible from state route 82 east out of Enterprise, where the Forest Service has a recreation headquarters.

2.) The entire Cascade Range in central Oregon is good mule deer country on the eastern slopes, especially in the Deschutes and Winema National Forests.

3.) The Blue Mountains east and west of LaGrande on I-80N in Union County produces plenty of big bucks.

Blacktail Deer

1.) One of the best areas for blacktails is along the central coast where 41 miles of scenic sand dunes afford hunters some rare open areas for hunting. This area is called the "Dunes" and stretches from the Siuslaw River near Florence southward to Coos Bay. Highway U. S. 101 provides excellent access to the Dunes National Recreation Area in the Siuslaw National Forest.

2.) Excellent blacktail deer hunting is found in the entire area surrounding Alson in Benton County west of U.S. 99. The forests surrounding Eugene and Corvallis have dense populations of blacktails.

Elk

The vast majority of elk in Oregon are found in the Oregon Coast Mountains and the western slopes of the Cascade Mountains. The northeastern corner of the state also has good elk hunting in the Blue Mountains, along with the extreme eastern part of the state along the Idaho line. There are lots of elk in Oregon, but there are also lots of people. In most areas of the state, hunting pressure is heavy.

1.) In the northern Coast Mountains, one of the best elk hunting areas is in the Wilson River area east of U.S. 101 in Tillamook County, and the Saddle Mountain area near Trask.

2.) The best southern Coast Mountain areas are in the mountains surrounding Eugene in Lane County. Another good area is the Coos River drainage east of Coos Bay on U.S. 101 in Coos County. The McKenzie River drainage east of Vida on U.S. 126 in Lane County is also good elk hunting, as is the north Umpqua River drainage east of Roseburg on I-5 in Douglas County of the Siskyou National Forest.

3.) In the northeastern corner, the Eagle Cap Wilderness Area is excellent for elk hunting. This area is in the Blue Mountains of the Wallowa-Whitman National Forest. Best spots are the Minam, Lostine, and Imnaha Rivers, as well as Eagle, Bear, and Big creeks. South of Wallowa in Wallowa County, another good spot in this area is the LaGrande area on U.S. 30 in Union County, especially in the LaGrande River drainage to the north.

4,) In the far eastern part of the state, the Hell's Canyon National Recreation Area along the Idaho border is a good producer of bull elk. This rugged area is accessible from state route 82 east to Enterprise, where the Forest Service has a recreation headquarters.

Mountain Lion

The best lion hunting in Oregon is around Roseburg and Medford, and in Douglas and Lane counties. Also, in the east along the Idaho border. A nonresident lion hunter should hire a guide with lion hounds. Lions are rarely seen without the aid of dogs.

Bighorn Sheep

About 100 sheep exist on Hart Mountain in Lake County. Transplants have also been made in the Owyhees, and the rugged Steens Mountains. Currently, only residents may apply for the handful of permits offered annually.

Rocky Mountain Goat

A small herd of goats resides in the Wallowa Mountains in the Eagle Cap Wilderness Area. Residents only may apply for the few permits issued annually.

Moose

Oregon has no viable moose population.

UTAH

Antelope

Utah has a small antelope herd, and only about 80 permits are issued each year. A serious antelope hunter would be wise to look to another western state that offers greater antelope hunting opportunities.

Black Bear

Utah has a small bear population, located mostly in the central part of the state in the Manti Mountain Range. Surprisingly, the current Boone and Crockett world record black bear came from the Manti Range.

1.) The best bet for bear hunting is in central Utah on the Wasatch Plateau, known locally as the Manti Range. The Manti Range is all public land and is part of the Manti-La Sal National Forest.

2.) Another good bear area in the Manti Range lies on the west slopes which include Oak and Birch Creeks east of Fairview in Sanpete County.

3.) In Sanpete County, another good bear hunting area lies in the upper reaches of Six Mile and Twelve Mile Canyons east of Sterling and Mayfield.

4.) The eastern slopes of the Manti Range receive less hunting pressure; one good bear area lies in the Muddy Creek and Big Bear Creek drainages west of Ferron in Emery County.

Mule Deer

Utah has a large and evenly distributed mule deer herd. State wildlife officials say that it's tough to pick a few spots in the state that are best, because they feel that it's good deer hunting throughout the state. The highest success rates come from the corners of the state, but the mountains east of Salt Lake City and Ogden produce a disproportionate number of big bucks along the Wasatch Front.

1.) In the southeastern corner of the state, excellent public hunting for muleys is found in the La Sal Mountains east of Moab on U.S. 160 in Grand County. This area is in the Manti-La Sal National Forest.

2.) In the north, the entire area along the Idaho border is prime muley country. A guide who works that country said that he would not be surprised to see the next world record mule deer come from that country.

3.) In the northwestern corner, western Box Elder County is one of the best areas for trophy size mule deer bucks, and hunters boast a 40% success rate. Specifically, try the Raft River Mountains along the Idaho border around Yost.

4.) There are lots of big muley bucks found in the Paunaugant hunting unit on the Paunaugant Plateau east of Panguitch on U.S. 89 in west Garfield County. This area is located next to Bryce Canyon National Park.

5.) In the southeastern part of the state, the San Juan-Elk Ridge hunting unit west of Monticello on U.S. 160 in east San Juan County is excellent for big mule deer bucks.

Elk

The Manti Range in central Utah has the best elk hunting. This area is located on the famous Wasatch Plateau in the Manti-La Sal National Forest. The elk herd in Utah has been steadily growing and branching out, and hunters in the near future can expect much more hunting potential from this state.

1.) One of the best areas is on the western slopes of the Manti Range in central Utah in Oak and Birch creeks east of Fairview on U.S. 89 in north Sanpete County. Another good spot is in the upper reaches of Six Mile and twelve Mile Canyons east of Sterling and Mayfield on U.S. 89 in South Sanpete County.

2.) The best elk hunting area on the east slopes of the Manti Range is in Huntington Canyon and the canyons above Joe's Valley, Muddy Creek, and Big Bear Creek west of Ferron on state route 10 in western Emery County. Another good spot in this area is the upper Fish Creek drainage east of Scofield Reservoir.

3.) In central Utah, elk in good numbers are found south of the Manti Range in the Fish Lake National Forest. Specifically, try the area south of state route 10 near Mount Hilgard and Mount Terrel in Sevier County.

Mountain Lion

The best mountain lion hunting is in the southwest corner of the state. A nonresident lion hunter should hire a guide with lion hounds. Lions are rarely seen in the wild without the aid of dogs.

Bighorn Sheep

There is a small herd of desert bighorns in San Juan County. Very limited hunting is allowed.

Rocky Mountain Goat

A small herd of goats resides in the mountains east of Salt Lake City between Big and Little Cottonwood Canyons. In the future, a few permits may be offered if this herd continues to grow.

Moose
There is a small, but growing, moose population in northern Utah on the north slopes of the Unita Mountains. Currently, residents receive most of the moose permits, but a few are issued to nonresidents.

WASHINGTON

Antelope

Even though eastern Washington has rolling prairie, antelope have not adapted well. Several transplants have failed, and today there is only a small herd of antelope living on the Yakima Federal Firing Range. No antelope hunting is planned for the near future.

Black Bear

The western half of Washington from the Cascade Mountains to the western coast is all prime bear habitat. Other good areas lie in the extreme northeast and southeast corners of the state.
1.) One of the best bear hunting areas lies in the rain forests south of the Strait of Juan De Fuca down along the western side of Olympic National Park. Bear densities in this region are very high.
2.) In the southern part of the state, the eastern slopes of the Cascade Mountains along the Naches River northeast of Yakima along U.S. 410 is a good place to hunt bears.
3.) In the southwest, the entire western side of the Cascade Range south of Mt. Rainier and south to the Oregon border is all excellent for hunting bears. The closer to the coast you go, the better the bear hunting gets.
4.) In the northwestern part of the state, the western slopes of the Cascades from the Canadian border south to Mt. Rainier National Park has a uniformly dense bear population.
5.) In the southeastern corner of the state, the Blue Mountains south of Dayton harbor a huntable population of black bears.
6.) In the northeastern corner of the state, the Kaniksu National Forest has excellent bear hunting north of Newport along the Idaho border in Pend Oreille County along state

highway 31.

Mule Deer

Mule deer inhabit the region east of the Cascade Mountain range, while blacktail, a subspecies of mule deer, inhabit the region on the western slopes of the Cascades.

1.) In the north, one of the best mule deer hunting areas is in the Paysayten Wilderness Area in the Cascade Mountains.

2.) In the northcentral part of the state, one of the most productive areas is Okanogan County, especially in the Chopaka Mountain area, or Chewak Creek north of Winthrop.

3.) In the southwest, the Mt. St.Helens area is excellent for mule deer hunting. The Gifford Pinchot National Forest to the east has a large and stable mule deer herd. Best bets are unit 560 along the Lewis River, and unit 516 near Packwood on state route 15 in Lewis County.

4.) In the southeast, the Blue Mountains south of Dayton have excellent mule deer hunting.

Blacktail

1.) Blacktail inhabit the western foothills of the Cascades west to the Coastal Mountains. The best counties for blacktail hunting are Lewis, Cowlitz, and Grays Harbor. There is a lot of public land to hunt in this area, and the blacktails are everywhere.

Whitetail

The heaviest concentrations of whitetail deer are in Pend Oreille and Stevens counties in the northeastern part of the state. However, whitetails will be found in every brushy creek bottom or sidehill in eastern Washington from the Canadian border south to Oregon. The best whitetail hunting units are unit-100 (Curlew), unit-109 (Gillette), unit-118 (Chewelah), 121 (Huckleberry).

Elk

Washington has a large elk herd, but it also has a lot of hunters in the field after them, and sometimes the pressure is intense in this populous state. Either/or hunting is now required, meaning you must choose to hunt during archery season or gun season, but not both.

1.) In the southcentral part of the state, the Yakima region is the biggest elk producer. The top areas are unit 356 (Bumping), 358 (Bumping-Bethel), 360 (Bethel), and 328 (Naneum).

2.) Excellent elk densities are found in the far western coastal region from the strait of Juan De Fuca all the way south to the Columbia River. The two top elk producers are unit 615 near Clearwater on U.S. 101 in Jefferson County just southwest of Olympic National Park, and unit 618 near Methany.

3.) Good elk hunting is found in the Mt. St. Helens region on the west slopes of the Cascades. Some of the best drainages for elk are the Cowlitz, Toutle, and Lewis rivers in Lewis and Cowlitz counties east of Columbia Heights on I-5. Other good areas in this region are unit-516 near Packwood on U.S. 14 in the upper Cowlitz River drainage, and unit-560 in the upper Lewis River drainage southeast of Spirit Lake.

4.) In the southeast, the Spokane region is located in the Blue Mountains. Unlike much of Washington's elk habitat, there is less brush in this area, and consequently hunters see more elk. In fact, this relatively small area has a harvest comparable to other regions that are much larger. The best areas are: unit-169 near Wenaha and unit-175 at Lickcreek.

5.) The Sound region covers the western slopes of the Cascades from the Canadian border down to the southwest corner of Mt. Rainier National Park. The best elk hunting area is in unit-472 in the White River drainage east of Enumclaw on U.S. 410 in King

County. Another good area is in unit-418 in the upper Nooksack River drainage northeast of Bellingham on I 5 in Whatcom County just below the Canadian border.

Mountain Lion

The best mountain lion hunting is done in a 150 square mile area in the northeast corner of the state in Pend Oreille and Stevens counties. A nonresident lion hunter should hire a guide with lion hounds. Lions are rarely seen in the wild without the aid of dogs.

Bighorn Sheep

There are about 200 bighorn sheep in Washington. They are scattered in small bands in the Sinlahekin Game Range in Okanogan County, the Tucannon Game Range in Columbia and Garfield counties, and the Clockum Game Range in Kittatis County. Only a few permits are issued annually.

Rocky Mountain Goat

The Cascade Mountain Range has a good goat population, and transplants have been made in the Olympic Mountains. Five of the top six goats in the Boone and Crockett record book have come from Washington, including the current world record. About 1,000 permits are issued annually and the goat kill runs about 400.

Moose

Moose are confined to the northeastern corner of the state in the Kaniksu National Forest in Pend Oreille County. A few permits are offered each year.

WYOMING

Antelope

Wyoming's best antelope range is found in the eastern half of the state, with some good hunting also located in the central part. A hunter can expect to find good antelope hunting anywhere in the open prairie country.

1.) In the northeastern corner of Wyoming, the counties of Campbell, Cook, and Weston are excellent for antelope hunting, and the ranches near Gillette, Sundance, and Newcastle are especially good.

2.) In the eastcentral part of the state, north of Douglas and Glenrock in Converse County is another good place to find big buck antelope. East of Douglas is also good all the way to Lusk on U.S. 20 and south along U.S. 85 to Torrington.

3.) No one can go wrong hunting antelope anywhere around Casper in Trona County.

4.) In the central part of the state, Lander in Fremont County, site of the famous One-Shot Antelope Extravaganza, is as good as any area in the state.

5.) The area west of Cheyenne on U.S. 30 in Laramie County to the Nebraska/Colorado border has good antelope density.

6.) The area northwest of Laramie in Albany County and southeast of Rawlins in Carbon County are two excellent antelope hunting areas known for producing trophy animals.

Black Bear

Wyoming has a small black bear population, mostly in the northern mountains. Lack of basic bear feed such as a fall berry crop keeps the bears from gaining in numbers.

1.) The best bet for bear hunting would be in the Absaroka Range east of Yellowstone National Park near the town of Pahaska along U.S. 14-20. Some of the best mountains to hunt are Castle, Silvertip, and Sunlight. This is grizzly country, so be sure of your target.

2.) Another decent bear hunting area is in the Wyoming Mountain Range between Alpine Junction and LaBarge. Specifically, look for bears along LaBarge Creek which runs north from LaBarge.

3.) In the north, the mountains surrounding Jackson, Cody, Atton, Pinedale, Dubois, and Saratoga are all good for bear hunting.

Mule Deer

The prime mule deer country is in the broad, forested area in the northwestern part of the state. The Bighorn National Forest in the northcentral and the Medicine Bow National Forest in the southeast are also good muley areas.

1.) In the northern part of the state, the Cabin Creek Camps about 16 miles northeast of Shell on U.S. 14 in Bighorn County is excellent for mule deer. Nearby Bruce Mountain and Bruce Creek are also good for muleys.

2.) In the northcentral part of the state, the Sheep Mountain area north of Route 16 is excellent for mule deer. This area is west of Story on U.S. 87 in Sheridan County. Other good spots in this area are Piney Creek, Penrose Mountain, and Little Goose Peak.

3.) In the northwest, there are lots of trophy class bucks in the mountains due east and south of Yellowstone National Park. Especially good are the Absaroka Mountains near Pahaska on U.S. 14-20 in Park County on the Shoshone National Forest.

4.) One of the best trophy mule deer areas is in the far west along the Idaho border near Afton on U.S. 89 in Lincoln County. The best drainage is the Greys River along the east side of the Salt River Range.

5.) In the western part of the state, the area east of Big Piney on U.S. 189 in Sublette County is excellent for mule deer in the Bridger National Forest. Specifically, try the Green River drainage and its side drainages northeast of Big Piney.

6.) There is top rated mule deer hunting in the Medicine Bow Mountains in the southcentral part of the state west of Hanna on U.S. 30-287 in Carbon County. Try the Medicine Bow River and Pass Creek drainage.

Whitetail Deer

The best whitetail hunting is located in the eastern and northeastern part of Wyoming in the river bottom country. The Black Hills National Forest around Sundance on U.S. 14 in Crook County is excellent for whitetails. Another good area is around New Castle and Moorcroft. One more good spot for whitetails is the Little Missouri River breaks north of Gillette.

Elk

The major elk populations are in the northwestern part of the state south and east of Yellowstone National Park, and in the northcentral area in the Bighorn National Forest. The top elk producing areas are in the Teton National Forest south of Yellowstone National Park and the Bridger National Forest southeast of Jackson in the western part of the state.

1.) Two major drainages in the Teton National Forest account for about one-third of the total elk kill in Wyoming. They are the Gros Ventre and Hoback River drainages in northwestern Wyoming south of the park. The Gros Ventre River drainage east of Kelly on U.S. 191 in Teton County is the top elk producing area in the state. The Hoback

—160—

drainage nearly matches the Gros Ventre in total elk harvest. It is located southeast of Jackson on U.S. 191 in Teton County.

2.) In the northwest part of the state, some of the largest concentrations of bull elk are found in the Absaroka Mountains east of Yellowstone National Park and west of Cody on both sides of U.S. 14-20. Besides a large resident elk herd, the Absaroka Mountains also accommodate a large migrating elk herd from the park each fall. The best areas are near peaks such as Castle, Cathedral, Silvertip, Sunlight, and Moose. The Manaco Camp up the craggy canyons of Moose Mountain is especially good.

3.) In the western part of the state, the Wyoming Mountain range of the Bridger National Forest is often overlooked but offers excellent elk hunting. This area extends between Alpine Junction on U.S. 89 in Sublette County to LaBarge on U.S. 189. Specifically, try Grayback Ridge and Cliff and LaBarge creeks, near Fontenelle Lakes, and by Mt. Isabel to the south. Other good areas are the Little Greys drainage, the Deadman Mountains, Blind Bull Canyon, and the heads of Grizzly and Cascade creeks.

4.) In the northcentral part of the state, the Bighorn National Forest is tops for elk hunting, especially in the mountains around Burgess Junction on U.S. 14 in Sheridan County.

5.) In the southcentral part of the state, the Medicine Bow National Forest west of Albany on state route 10 in Carbon County is a very good elk hunting area. Specifically, try the area around Saratoga Springs east of Wislope on state route 130.

Mountain Lion

The Bighorn Mountains offer the top lion hunting in Wyoming. A nonresident lion hunter should hire a guide with lion hounds. Lions are rarely seen in the wild without the aid of dogs.

Bighorn Sheep

Wyoming has a substantial population of sheep in the western mountain ranges. Prime sheep areas are the Bighorn Mountains, and the Laramie Peak area of the Medicine Bow National Forest. About 400 permits are issued annually, and 25% of those go to nonresidents. Hunter success is 40%. Other regions with good sheep populations and high kills are Jakey's Fork of the Green River in the lower part of the Shoshone National Forest. The Crescent Mountain region of the Continental Divide north and west of Dubois, and the mountain country east of Jackson in the Gros Ventre drainage are also good sheep county.

Rocky Mountain Goat

Only a small population of goats inhabit Wyoming in the northwestern part of the state north of Clark's Fork River. This is the Beartooth Pass region reached out of Cooke City. Only a handful of permits are issued annually, but 25% go to nonresidents.

Moose

Some of the best moose areas are on the east and south sides of Yellowstone National Park in the Shoshone and Teton National Forests.

1.) The upper Green River country is probably the best area for moose in Wyoming (units 3,4,5). Also, the Green River proper is fine moose country in units 24 and 25.

2.) Moose are found in good numbers in the level valley of the lower Green River, and along such tributaries as the New Fork Creek, Cottonwood Creek, and Gypsum Creek.

3.) The biggest bull moose are found in the Wyoming Range of mountains between Alpine Junction and LaBarge in the Shoshone National Forest.

Appendix B

ADDRESSES

The following list of addresses covers three areas: state wildlife agencies, regional U.S. Forest Service offices, and topographical map source. Use these addresses to pin-point a specific hunting spot.

State Wildlife Agencies

Arizona Game and Fish Department
2222 W. Greenway Road
Phoenix, Arizona 85023
(602) 942-3000

Colorado Division of Wildlife
6060 Broadway
Denver, Colorado 85023
(303) 297-1192

Idaho Fish and Game Department
600 S. Walnut
Boise, Idaho 83707
(208) 334-3700

Montana Dept. of Fish, Wildlife, Parks
1420 East Sixth
Helena, Montana 59620
(406) 444-2535

Nevada Department of Wildlife
P.O. Box 10678
Reno, Nevada 89520
(702) 784-6214

New Mexico Game and Fish Dept.
Villagre Building
Santa Fe, New Mexico 87503
(505) 827-2923

Oregon Dept. of Fish and Wildlife
P.O. Box 3503
Portland, Oregon 97208
(503) 229-5551

Utah Division of Wildlife Resources
1596 W.N. Temple
Salt Lake City, Utah 84116
(801) 533-9333

Washington Dept. of Game
600 N. Capitol Way
Olympia, Washington 98504
(206) 753-5700

Wyoming Game and Fish Dept.
Cheyenne, Wyoming 82002
(307) 777-7631

U.S. Forest Service

Below are the regional offices of the Forest Service. You can obtain specific information and maps from them for a particular National Forest.

Region 1 (Montana, Northern Idaho)
Federal Building
Missoula, Montana 59807
(406) 329-3316

Region 2 (Colorado, part of Wyoming)
11177 W. 8th Avenue
P.O. Box 25127
Lakewood, Colorado 80225
(303) 234-3711

Region 3 (Arizona, New Mexico)
Federal Building
517 Gold Avenue S.W.
Albuquerque, New Mexico 87102
(505) 766-2401

Region 4 (Nevada, Utah, Southern Idaho, Western Wyoming)
Federal Building
324 25th Street
Ogden, Utah 84401
(801) 626-3201

Region 6 (Oregon, Washington)
319 S.W. Pine Street
P.O. Box 3623
Portland, Oregon 97208
(503) 221-3625

Topographic Maps

First ask for free state order maps, and then from them order the specific state, regional, county, or quadrangle topographic maps to cover your hunting area.

Branch of Distribution
U.S. Geological Survey
Federal Center
Denver, Colorado 80225
(303) 234-3832

Appendix C

Additional Sources

Below is a list of recommended books and videos to better prepare the nonresident hunter for his upcoming western big game hunt. Books and videos are available from: Stoneydale Press, 205 Main Street, Drawer B, Stevensville, MT. 59870

Books

1.) *Successful Big Game Hunting* (elk, mule deer, whitetail, Coues deer, bear, sheep, goats, moose, antelope.) by Duncan Gilchrist
2.) *Elk Hunting In The Northern Rockies*, by Ed Wolff
3.) *Bugling For Elk*, by Dwight Schuh
4.) *Bowhunting For Mule Deer*, by Dwight Schuh
5.) *Taking Big Bucks: Solving the Whitetail Riddle*, by Ed Wolff
6.) *Montana Hunting Guide*, by Dale Burk
7.) *Complete Guide To Field Care Of Trophies*, by Duncan Gilchrist
8.) *Oregon Hunting Guide*, by John A. Johnson
9.) *Radical Elk Hunting Strategies*, by Mike Lapinski
10.) *Dale Burk's Pocket Guide Series - Whitetail Deer, Mule Deer, Elk Hunting, Elk Calling, Black Bear, Moose, Mountain Goat, Antelope*, by various authors

Videos

Rocky Mountain Elk, Their Life Story
Rocky Mountain Bighorn Sheep, Their Life Story
Elk Hunting In The Rocky Mountain West
Hunting Trophy Whitetails
Caping And Field Dressing Big Game
Early Season Elk Hunting
Hunting Rocky Mountain Mule Deer
Hunting Trophy Whitetails
Planning Your Rocky Mountain Hunt
Secrets of Hunting Black Bear
Scoring North American Big Game Trophies